A Daybook for February

in Yellow Springs, Ohio

A Memoir in Nature

**and a Handbook for the Month,
Being a Personal Narrative and Synthesis of
Common Events in Nature
between 1981 and 2023
in Southwestern Ohio, with Applications
for the Lower Midwest and Middle Atlantic
Region, Containing Weather Guidelines
and a Variety of Natural Calendars,
Reflections by the Author
and Seasonal Quotations
from Ancient and Modern Writers**

By

Bill Felker

A Daybook for the Year in Yellow Springs, Ohio
Volume 2: February
Cover from a watercolor by Libby Rudolf

Copyright 2023by Bill Felker
Published by The Green Thrush Press
P.O. Box 431, Yellow Springs, Ohio

Printed in the United States of America

ISBN-9781726835084

For Neysa

No one suspects the days to be gods.

Ralph Waldo Emerson

Introduction

Find a portion of the raw world that is nearby. Adopt it.... No matter how small an area it may be, it creates particular harmonics that ripple across your common time and space. The degree of your sincerity of concerns draws taut the weave, creating a four-dimensional tapestry: Nature, time, space, and you.

Peter London, *Drawing Closer to Nature*

*This collection is like a diary of my expeditions, which makes me set out again with renewed joy..... It is the chain of **accessory ideas** that makes me love botany. It brings together and recalls to my imagination all the images which most charm it: meadows, waters, woods, solitude and above all the peace and tranquility which one can find in these places – all of this it instantly conjures up before my memory.*

Jean-Jacques Rousseau, on his herbarium in *Reveries of the Solitary Walker* (Translation: Peter France)

After my family and I moved to southwestern Ohio in 1978, I began to hike in the woods and fields. As I walked, I took notes about flowers blooming, trees leafing, birds calling, insects crawling.

Exploring and writing about what was happening in the natural world became a habit and a way of life, and for the past 45 years, I have kept records of the progress of the seasons in my hometown of Yellow Springs and in the surrounding area of the Ohio Valley.

A personal practice of watching has taken different paths through the years. At first, an investigation of botany and taxonomy rewarded my walks with the names of the plants and trees that I saw. Then there were insects to name and follow, and birds.

As a way of compiling and sorting this information, I put together a daybook. This book has one chapter for each day of the year, and each chapter contains my notes of that day for most years between 1978 and 2023. It has become a teacher that has shown me how clusters of observations create seasons as well as places. It has also been a reference for personal and local natural history.

Among the many rewards of this process is a growing perception of the time and space of my own narrow habitat. What has fascinated me most recently is that the elements or signs of time are also the building blocks of place, a perspective I had always taken for granted.

I learn that the year and the location observed take on their character from those signs, or what anthropologist Keith Basso calls "mnemonic pegs." I see that I might use such pegs (formed by objects or events like sprouting crocuses or singing birds) to formulate a "topogeny," a collection of phenomena that creates maps or paths.

Like the technique of singing the names of landmarks for navigation, used by the aboriginal inhabitants of Australia and described by Bruce Chatwin in *The Songlines*, the naming of and relationship with the flora and fauna, in the context of home, can form a sequence of markers with which to plot consciousness, passage and location and so to understand when and where I am.

I begin to see how the landscape and the climate of my village of Yellow Springs are the sum of their parts (of their mnemonic pegs), and that keeping track of them brings them into existence for me, showing me the way. And the simple process of watching common phenomena brings about a sort of ongoing conversion in the way I look at everything.

I also see that a portion of the "raw world" that Peter London urged his readers to adopt ("a four-dimensional tapestry: Nature, time, space, and you*")* does not exclude the wider world. Rather, it serves as a gauge for what lies beyond it, introducing and enhancing it, putting it in an immediate context, giving it relevance. This world that I record here leads outward as well as inward, and it is a guide that unlocks a beginner's mind.

These days, I realize, too, as Rousseau did, that there is great enjoyment just in seeing where I have been and in reliving the experiences, realizing that going back over them makes me happy. I have slowed down quite a bit since I began this pilgrimage. My habitat has become even smaller, and the daybook compensates, connects me to an endless number of spaces and times that accumulate and mix with impressions, memories and "accessory ideas" to form another dimension.

Like Rousseau, I live again in this way of nature, my thoughts both linear and radial, binding together consciousness of years past with birdcalls and the length of leaves and the opening of flowers.

Finally, all of this has led me to view my practice as an examples of what Suzanne Simard, echoing Peter London, has suggested as a way to fight for the survival of the planet.

Despite the gathering Anthropocene, "we have the power to shift course," Simard challenges the reader in her book, *Finding the Mother Tree*. "It's up to each and every one of us. Connect with plants you can call your own. If you're in a city, set a pot on your balcony. If you have a yard, start a garden or join a community plot. Here's a simple and profound action you can take right now: go find a tree--*your tree*. Imagine linking into her network, connecting to other trees nearby. Open your senses.... Turning to the intelligence of *nature itself* is the key."

The Daybook Format

The format of my notes in this daybook owes more than a little to the almanacs I wrote for the *Yellow Springs News* between 1984 and 2023. The quotations, daily statistics, the weather outlooks, the seasonal calendar, and the daybook entries were and still are part of my regular routine of collecting and organizing impressions about the place in which I live.

Setting: The principal habitat described here is that of Glen Helen, a preserve of woods and glades that lies on the eastern border of the village of Yellow Springs in southwestern Ohio. At its northern edge, the Glen joins with John Bryan State Park to form a corridor about ten miles long, and half a mile wide, along the Little Miami River. The north section of the Glen Helen /John Bryan complex is hilly and heavily wooded, and is the best location for spring wildflowers. The southern portion, "South Glen" as it is usually called, is a combination of open fields, wetlands, and wooded flatlands. Here I found many flowers and grasses of summer and fall. Together, the two Glens and John Bryan Park provide a remarkable cross section of the fauna and flora of the eastern United States.

Other habitats in the daybook include my yard with its several small gardens; the village of Yellow Springs itself, a town of 4,000 at the far eastern border of the Dayton suburbs; the Caesar Creek Reservoir, twenty miles south of Yellow Springs and created by the Corps of Engineers in 1976. My trips away from that environment were principally northeast to Chicago, Madison, Wisconsin and northern Minnesota, east to Washington and New York, southeast to the Carolinas and Florida, southwest to Arkansas, Louisiana, and Texas, and occasionally through the Southwest to California and the Northwest, two excursions to Belize in Central America, several to Italy.

Quotations: The passages from ancient and modern writers (and sometimes from my alter egos) which accompany each day's notations are lessons from my readings, as well as from distant seminary and university training, here put to work in service of the reconstruction of my sense of time and space. They are a collection of reminders, hopes, and promises for me that I find implicit in the seasons. They have also become a kind of a cosmological scrapbook for me, as well as the philosophical underpinning of this narrative.

Astronomical Data: The *Daybook* includes approximate dates for astronomical events, such as star positions, meteor showers, solstice, equinox, perihelion (the Sun's position closest to earth), and aphelion (the Sun's position farthest from Earth).

I have included the sunrise and sunset for Yellow Springs as a general guide to the progression of the year in this location, but those statistics also reflect trends that are world wide, if more rapid in some places and slower in others.

Even though the day's length is almost never exactly the same from one town to the next, a minute gained or lost in Yellow Springs is often a minute lost or gained elsewhere, and the Yellow Springs numbers can be used as a simple way of watching the lengthening or shortening of the days, and, therefore, of watching the turn of the planet. For those who wish to keep track of the Sun themselves in their own location, abundant sources are now available for this information in local and national media.

Average Temperatures: Average temperatures in Yellow Springs are also part of each day's entry. Since the rise and fall of temperatures in other parts of the North America, even though they may start from colder or warmer readings, keep pace with the temperatures here, the highs and lows in Yellow Springs are, like solar statistics, helpful indicators of the steady progress of the year throughout most of the states along the 40th Parallel (except in the mountains). The daybook entries can be cross-referenced with the list of monthly average temperatures between 1981 and 2017 in order to compare the daily inventories with the month's weather in a given year.

Weather: My daily, weekly and monthly weather summaries have been distilled from over thirty years of observations. They are descriptions of the local weather history I have kept in order to track the gradual change in temperatures, precipitation and cloud cover through the year I have also used them in order to try to identify particular characteristics of each day. They are not meant to be predictions.

Although my interest in the Yellow Springs microclimate at first seemed too narrow to be of use to those who lived outside the area, I began to modify it to meet the needs of a number of regional and national farm publications for which I started writing in the mid 1980s. And so, while the summaries are based on my records in southwestern Ohio, they can be and have been used, with interpretation and interpolation, throughout the Lower Midwest , the Middle Atlantic States and the East.

The Natural Calendar: In this section, I note the progress of foliage and floral changes, farm and garden practices, migration times for common birds, and peak periods of insect activity. Some of these notes are second hand; I'm a sky watcher, but not an astronomer, and I rely on the government's astronomical data and a few other references for much of my information about the stars and the sun. I am also a complete amateur at bird watching, and most of the migration dates used in the seasonal calendar come from published sources. And even though I keep close track of the farm year, the percentages listed for planting and harvesting are interpretations of averages supplied by the state's weekly crop reports.

Daybook Entries: The entries in the daybook section provide the raw material from which I wrote the Natural Calendar digests. The daybook section is a collection of observations made from the window of my car and from my walks in Glen Helen, in parks and wildlife areas within a few miles of my home, and on occasional trips. It is a record that anyone with a few guidebooks could make, and it includes just a small number of the natural markers that anyone might discover.

When I began to take notes about the world around me, I found that there were few descriptions of actual events in nature available for southwestern Ohio. There was no roadmap for the course of the year. My daily observations, as narrow and incomplete as they were, were especially significant to me since I had found no other narrative of the days, no other depiction of what was actually occurring around me. In time, the world came into focus with each particle I named. I saw concretely that time and space were the sum of their parts.

As my notes for each day accumulated, I could see the wide variation of events that occurred from year to year; at the same time, I saw a unity in this syncopation from which I could identify numerous sub-seasons and with which I could understand better the kind of habitat in which I was living and, consequently, myself.

When I paged through the entries for each day, I was drawn back to the space in which they were made. I browsed and imagined, returned to the journey.

Journal Essays: At the end of many of the daybook entries, I have included brief essays from my almanac column in the *Yellow Springs News*.

Companions: Many friends, acquaintances and family members have contributed their observations to the daybook, and their participation has taught me that my private seasons are also community seasons, and that all of our experiences together help to lay the foundation for a rich, local consciousness of natural history.

February Averages: 1981 through 2023
Normal February Average Temperature: 31

Year	Average
1981	32.9
1982	27.6
1983	34.4
1984	36.3
1985	25.3
1986	31.3
1987	34.1
1988	27.1
1989	27.5
1990	37.3
1991	34.9
1992	36.3
1993	26.3
1994	28.8
1995	28.1
1996	30.2
1997	35.0
1998	39.2
1999	35.7
2000	36.7
2001	34.1
2002	34.7
2003	24.7
2004	30.7
2005	33.3
2006	31.6
2007	18.4
2008	28.2
2009	32.1
2010	24.7
2011	31.5
2012	36.0
2013	30.5
2014	24.2
2015	20.4
2016	33.4
2017	41.8
2018	37.1
2019	34.8
2020	33.9
2021	25.9
2022	32.8
2023	40.9

February 1st
The 32nd Day of the Year

*Now learn the signs
Of cold and heat to come,
Of drought and rain,
The secrets of the moon,
And what each wind will bring.*

Virgil

Sunrise/set 7:44/5:54
Day's Length: 10 hours 10 minutes
Average High/Low: 35/19
Average Temperature: 27
Record High: 60 – 1986
Record Low: - 5 – 1929

Weather

High temperatures rise to the 60s five percent of the years, reach above 50 fifteen percent, and into the 40s on 25 percent of the years. Colder conditions also come on this date: 30s twenty-five percent of the time, 20s fifteen percent, and teens another fifteen percent. Skies are generally cloudy: today and the 3rd are the most overcast of the month, bringing only a 35 percent chance of sun. Rain or snow falls half of the years, and thunderstorms are more likely to occur today and tomorrow than on any other days in February.

The Week Ahead

The first two days of February often bring mild temperatures in the 50s and 60s to the Lower Midwest, the Middle Atlantic Region and the East. Beginning on the 3rd, however, conditions typically become chillier: the likelihood for below-zero temperatures becomes the greatest of the entire winter, and the chances of highs just in the 30s or below remains steady at 60 percent. The second barometric high arrives near the 6th and generally redoubles the cold. The driest days of February's first quarter are the 7th and 8th, each bringing just a 20 percent chance of rain or snow. The wettest are 1st (with a 55 percent chance of precipitation), and the 3rd, and 6th (each with a 40 percent chance). The sunniest day, with almost a 70 percent chance of at least partly cloudy skies, is the 4th.

Columbian Almanack for 1789

Normal February average temperatures climb six degrees in and around Yellow Springs. Starting in the upper 20s, they rise one degree every 120 hours, reaching the middle 30s by the first of March.

A typical February brings one day with highs in the 60s, two or three in the 50s, a week in the 40s, eight to ten days in the 30s, six in the 20s and one or two days only in the teens or single digits. There is a 50 percent chance of a morning or two below zero.

The coldest part of February usually falls between the 1st and the 14th. Early Spring, a pivotal warming time, occurs by the 17th seven years out of ten. Wildflower foliage begins to appear; bulbs push up; buds swell on the trees; groundhogs and opossums become more active.

The February days with at least a forty percent chance of highs only in the 20s or below are the 4th, 5th, 6th, 7th, 8th, and 12th. The warmest days, those with a thirty percent chance of highs above 50, are the 2nd, 15th, 18th, 19th, 21st, 22nd, 23rd, and 28th. The 22nd is typically the warmest day of all, having a 50 percent chance of highs above 50 degrees.

The normal precipitation for February (in water equivalent) is 2.11 inches, the second lowest of the year. The wettest February days, those with at least a 50 percent chance of precipitation, are the 1st, 3rd, 6th, 11th, 14th, 15th, and 21st. Snow is most likely to fall on the 3rd through the 6th, on the 11th and 12th, and the 25th.

The driest February days, those that bring a twenty percent chance or less for precipitation, are the 7th, 8th, 10th, and 20th. The percent of possible sunshine increases four percent from that of January, up to 45 percent. The sunniest February days, those with at least a 60 percent chance of sun, are the 4th, 23rd, 26th, 27th, and 28th. The days that have at least a 60 percent chance of clouds are the 1st, 3rd, 6th, 11th, 14th, 16th, 17th, 19th, 21st, and 22nd.

Between six and eight major banks of high pressure move across the Midwest this month. The first four February weather systems belong to the subseason of Late Winter, the last three to Early Spring. Frozen precipitation usually precedes these fronts except between February 17th and 23rd, when the amount of snow often decreases to November levels.

Springcount

Twenty-three major spring cold fronts cross the Ohio Valley between the middle of February and the last week of May. The first three weather systems come this month. Although they can sometimes be just as chilling as the winter fronts, Early Spring systems are usually followed by more telling warm spells that gradually bring changes to the local flora.

February 3: As the final front of January weakens, it often brings the brief "Groundhog Day Thaw," a warm spell often potent enough to bring skunk cabbage into bloom as far north as the Great Lakes. February 3rd, however, consistently pushes a strong high-pressure ridge across the Mississippi, sharply raising the possibility of below-zero temperatures, and initiating a weeklong period of increased possibilities for bitter daytime highs. Precipitation is to be expected before the arrival of this front, and February 3rd is one of the February days most likely to bring dangerous storms to the Plains and tornadoes to the South. After the passage of this system, skies become clear three days out of four, but the sun seldom means warmer afternoons.

February 6: The second barometric high of February arrives near the 6th and generally reinforces the cold. The next three days frequently bring dangerous weather to the nation's midsection and produce some of the most frigid mornings of the entire year. Precipitation typically is low after this high-pressure wave crosses the country.

February 11: The third cold wave of the month, ordinarily the last severe system of Late Winter, arrives near this date, bearing a high chance of precipitation and sunless skies. And as this system moves east, the odds for milder weather become substantial.

February 15: Although the February 15th high-pressure ridge can be disappointing to those most in need of spring, the aftermath of this cold wave brings increasing odds for the best thaw so far in the year. Since mild winds from the Gulf of Mexico are likely to clash with Arctic air during this period, however, the days between the 14th and 18th bring an increased likelihood of storms.

February 20: Weather history is kind to the February 20th front. Although high pressure does sweep across the nation near this date, the low that precedes that front often brings some of the warmest temperatures of the month. Even when it passes through, the system rarely brings major difficulties to travelers or farmers. And as the barometer drops before the next front, it sometimes makes the 22nd and 23rd some of the most gentle days since early December.

February 24: After the benign days of February's third week that often force snowdrops and aconites into bloom, the chilly February 24th front almost always pushes Snowdrop Winter deep into the South. Since this high often clashes strongly with the moist air of Early Spring, snowstorms, flooding and tornadoes are more likely to occur now than at any time since the 15th. The 26th, or the day after this high pressure passes through, however, is dry and partly cloudy most of the time, and the 27th is usually mild as low-pressure precedes the end-of-the-month high.

February 27: This front is almost always more gentle than the February 24th front, and its transit signals the end of Snowdrop

Winter. Clear skies are a hallmark of this front's arrival, and bright conditions usually follow on the 28th.

The Four Phases of February

One way to look at February weather in the Lower Midwest is to divide it into four basic weather phases; even though each phase is different in each part of the country, the general pattern holds true most years:

Phase 1: The Groundhog Day Thaw between January 31st and February 3rd.
Phase 2: The last and often coldest days of winter between the 4th and 16th
Phase 3: The beginning of Early Spring and a softening of conditions throughout the country between the 17th and the 23rd
Phase 4: A return of colder weather between the 24th and March 7th

Key to the Nation's Weather

The typical February temperature at average elevations along the 40th Parallel, the average of the high of 40 and the low of 21, is 31 degrees. Using the following chart based on weather statistics from around the country, one can calculate the approximate temperatures in other locations close to the cities listed.

For example, starting from the base of "0," you can estimate normal temperatures in Burlington by subtracting 13 degrees from the base average. Or add 14 degrees to find out the likely conditions in Raleigh during the month.

Minneapolis MN	-15
Burlington VT	-13
Des Moines IA	-7
Chicago IL	-3
Pittsburg PA	-2
Boston MA	-1
AVERAGE ALONG 40th PARALLEL	31
New York, NY	+5
St. Louis MO	+6

Louisville KY	+8
Washington DC	+9
Atlanta GA	+18
New Orleans LA	+28
Miami FL	+39

A Floating Sequence
for the Blooming of Shrubs, Trees, Wildflowers and Perennials

A floating chronology is a sequence of events whose dates are all known in relation to one another, yet the time when the sequence as a whole occurred is unknown.

Martin Gorst, *Measuring Eternity*

The following list is based on my personal observations in southwestern Ohio over a period of 30 years. The dates are approximate, but I have tried to show a relatively true sequence of first blossoming times during an average spring.

Although the dates on all flower calendars are somewhat arbitrary (and may vary by more than 60 days between the Canadian border and the South), a "floating calendar" can be used throughout the country by adjusting the sequence to fit the climate.

For example, if snowdrops bloom at a particular location on March 20 instead of February 20, all the following blooming dates will follow more or less in the order given, but on later dates in average years.

February 2:	Skunk Cabbage (*Symplocarpus foetidus*)
February 18:	Snowdrop (*Galanthus nivalis*)
	Aconite *(Eranthis)*
February 22:	Snow Crocus (*Cocus chrysanthus*)
February 23:	*Iris Reticulata*
February 25	Silver Maple (*Acer saccharinum*)
February 28	Red Maple *(Acer rubrum)*
March 3:	Baby Blue Eyes or Gray Field Speedwell (*Veronica polita*)
March 4:	Common Chickweed (*Stellaria media*)
March 5:	Small-Flowered Bittercress

	(*Cardamine parviflora*)
March 7	Early Dogwood (*Cornus mas)*
March 8:	Snow Trillium (*Trillium nivale*)
March 9:	Purple Deadnettle (*Lamium purpureum*)
March 10:	Mid-Season Crocus
March 11:	Dandelion (*Taraxacum*)
March 12:	Scilla (*Scilla siberica*)
March 15:	Early Daffodils (*Narcissus*)

February Phenology

When titmouse make its early mating calls, then farmers test cattle for anaplasmosis.

When red-winged blackbirds arrive in the Lower Midwest, then the maple sap should already be running there. In Arizona, the hay harvest will be underway, and farmers in California will be planting the spring oats and barley.

When the first snowdrops emerge from their foliage (but are still not open, then sprout cabbages, kale, and collards under lights.

When aconites bloom, then gardeners and farmers spread fertilizer in the field and garden so that it can work its way into the ground before planting.

When the Groundhog Day thaw arrives, then skunk cabbage is starting bloom across the wetlands

When the first daffodil foliage is two inches tall in Midwestern gardens, then monarch butterflies begin to migrate north from Mexico.

When sparrows are courting, then branches of forsythia and pussy willows are cut for forcing indoors.

When pussy willows are half-emerged, then it is time to spray fruit trees with dormant oil. Include ash, bittersweet, fir, elm, hawthorn, juniper, lilac, linden, maple, oak, pine, poplar, spruce, sweet gum, tulip tree and willow for scales and mites.

When the first knuckles of rhubarb emerge from the ground, then it's time to plant onion sets directly in the ground and to seed cold frames with spinach, radishes and lettuce.

When you skunks come out at night, then geraniums, impatiens and coleus are seeded under lights for May and June.

When the red tips of peonies push out just a little from

the ground, then blue jays are courting and wild turkeys to are gathering in flocks.

When strawberry plants have new foliage, then the steelhead salmon run, which started in the fall, finally comes to a close in Lake Erie.

When wild multiflora roses sprout their first leaves in the Ohio Valley, then wildflower season has begun in the Southwest and bald eagles are laying their eggs in Yellowstone.

When tulip foliage emerges from the ground in the Lower Midwest, then horned owlets hatch in the woods and sweet corn is coming up along the Gulf coast. Redbuds and azaleas are in full bloom in Georgia, rhododendrons just starting to come in. In the lowlands of Mississippi, swamp buttercups are open, violets and black medic, too.

When small brown moths on appear on warmer afternoons, then ducks are looking for nesting sites and salamanders are mating at night in the slime.

Natural Calendar

In the first week of February, natural history shows the growing power of the spring. Like the steady shifting of the Sun north, precedents make promise and potential for the fledgling season.

Almost every year, Skunk Mating Season begins in the Groundhog Day Thaw. Salamander Breeding Season opens in the first mild rains, and the bobbing blue jays announce Blue Jay Courting Season. Doves called occasionally throughout December and January; now the Dove Calling Season swells with the predawn songs of cardinals and titmice. Throughout the Lower Midwest, deer move into herds for Deer Gathering in Herds Season.

Four months ahead of the Ohio Valley, Firefly Season starts in southern Florida. Along the Gulf of Mexico, Violet, Wintersweet, Winter Honeysuckle, Lenten Rose, Strawberry and Jasmine Blooming Seasons have begun. In northern Mexico, Monarch Butterfly Migration Season brings the surviving monarchs toward the Texas border. They will arrive in the United States during mid to late March, and their offspring will find the Midwest in Middle Summer.

By ten o'clock in the evening in the first week in February, Orion has moved west from its dominating January position in the center of the southern sky. The star grouping of Canis Major takes its place along the horizon, with Sirius, the Dog Star, the brightest star in the whole night sky.

Daybook

1981: Ducks on the open river, downy woodpeckers in the trees, a hawk circling, starlings in the mock orange.

1986: Large flock of geese flies over at 4:08 p.m. New mint leaves picked in South Glen.

1988: At 8:30 this morning, I heard a dove calling. Still no early cardinals, though. Thunder in the rain, 10:22 a.m., and also this afternoon, and then after dark. David Jensen's and Jane Morgan's snowdrops were blooming in the Vale today.

1989: Cardinal sings at 7:23 a.m. Three robins seen in the yard. Yellow crocus fully open in the yard, daffodils budding at Gail's bookstore downtown.

1992: Three daffodils are two inches high at the bookstore.

1993: First doves of the year heard at Wilberforce, 7:50 a.m. The cardinals and blue jays are still quiet, winter giving way reluctantly. But then I found a ladybug crawling up the window in the library.

1998: Juncos seen along Wilberforce Clifton Road this noon.

1999: Cold and rain for the Groundhog Day Thaw. Daffodils in the east garden are up an inch or two, close to the house. The garlic in the round garden has come back, now leads the daffodils by an inch.

2002: Camelback cricket found in the bathtub when I got up. Skunk odor in the back yard at 6:00 a.m. The daisy-like "little blooming geese" flowers were blooming in Susi's lawn today.

2003: Blue jays and robins at South Glen, the background chatter of the birds picking up.

2006: First cardinals sang at 7:25 this morning. Doves began at 7:28, and crows flew over at 7:30. The temperature was just below freezing, and the sunrise was red.

2008: Sleet and rain and snow, temperature holding in the middle 30s, flooding in the yard and across the front sidewalk. The birds feed hard, and a flock of goldfinches is in the garden, clustered up to seven at a time on the thistle socks.

2011: I woke to ice everywhere this morning. The day was raw but uneventful, then light rain or sleet began at about 4:00 this afternoon. Blizzard conditions predicted for Chicago tonight, a "storm of the century." Rick writes: "Hey Bill, Ten o'clock Tues. night, flashes of lightning, sirens howling like coyotes on the desert, branches cracking like rifle shots, ice crashing down all over the place! I'm about to look in Poor Will's Almanack and see if you have anything to do with this. Everyone home, no cars on the road. "

2012: Another near record-breaking day, the high at 58 as I write this in the middle of the afternoon. Some snowdrops on the south side of the front walk have emerged far enough to hang ready to open, Liz's snowdrops are a little ahead of ours, and the patch of aconites is brighter but still not blooming. About a fourth of our pussy willows have emerged about half way. Crows came by at 7:31 this morning, and the blue jay on Limestone Street was calling early, sparrows chattering, too, but still no cardinal songs either in the morning or in the afternoon. Many more crows than usual reported in downtown Springfield, up to 100,000 according to Wayne Baker on the radio.

2013: Cold in the single digits this morning, cardinal singing outside my window in the twilight, 7:12 a.m., an exact half an hour before sunrise.

2014: Mild and misting: the morning silent until crows burst out calling at 7:18. Then cardinals from 7:22 on. When I went out to feed birds in the yard, I came across deer scat and tracks in the snow.

2015: All of the forecasts called for cold and snow today, but the storm went north. Judy got eight to ten inches of snow and bitter winds in Goshen, Indiana, just 150 miles from Yellow Springs. Here, just mild temperatures in the upper 30s and light rain. So the Groundhog Day Thaw materialized when I thought there was no chance of it coming.

2016: A soft, gray morning in the upper 30s: cardinal call notes ("chits") heard in the honeysuckles at 7:17, male cardinal call at 7:19, crows around 7:30. In the dooryard garden, the first two snowdrops have started to bend, white tips extending. By late afternoon, there were five. Liz sent a message: she saw her second yellow-bellied sapsucker of the year today, had seen her first in the last days of January.

2018: Hard winter cold came in this afternoon with wind and sailing cumulus clouds. At the pond outside of town, geese by the hundreds and hundreds.

2019: Five inches of snow overnight. A robin in the front honeysuckle. A vague odor of skunk spreads throughout the east half of the house. As I walked Ranger, my border collie, about 9:00 this evening, a large flock of geese flew somewhere over to the west end of town, calling, honking.

2023: Sun and cold in the teens this morning, an inch of snow on the ground, Jill's and the Danielsons' aconites tucked in abeyance. In the Southeast, severe ice storms.

The bud stands for all things,
even for those things that don't flower,
for everything flowers, from within, of self-blessing;
though sometimes it is necessary

to reteach a thing its loveliness,
to put a hand on its brow
of the flower
and retell it in words and in touch
it is lovely
until it flowers again from within, of self-blessing;

Galway Kinnell, "Saint Francis and the Sow"

Foul weather is no news; hail, rain, and snow
Are now expected, and esteemed no woe;
Nay, 'tis an omen bad, the yeomen say
When Phoebus shows his face the second day.

The Country Almanack, February 1676

Sunrise/set: 7:43/5:55
Day's Length: 10 hours 12 minutes
Average High/Low: 35/19
Average Temperature: 27
Record High: 65 – 1903
Record Low: - 16 – 1951

Weather

Today is often is the mildest day of the first two weeks of February (the peak of the brief Groundhog Day Thaw), with highs in the 50s twenty-five percent of the time, and 40s thirty-five percent. Cooler 30s occur 20 percent of the days, 20s on 15 percent and teens on five percent. Skies are overcast half the time, and carry rain or snow 35 percent of the years.

Natural Calendar

The Groundhog Day Thaw gets underway by the 1st of February as the last cold front of January moves east. Thunderstorms can make their appearance with that thaw, and the temperature of the earth sometimes surges well above 40 degrees, telling the pastures to start growing.

In the gentle, wet nights around Groundhog Day, you will catch the first whiff of spring skunk. In the daytime, you can pick new mint leaves in the woods, and find the pale Asian lady bugs emerging in the sun all around your house.

Robins and bluebirds arrived the last week of January. Now juncos are flocking all along the backroads, getting ready for their migration north. Sparrows are mating, and the great morning chorus that lasts deep into summer is well underway, the starlings whistling and chattering by a quarter to eight, the crows and cardinals and doves joining in. Male blue jays are bobbing up and down, talking to their mates.

By the 12th, the day's length is a full hour longer than it was on December 26th, and the brighter afternoons tell the groundhogs and opossums that it's mating time. Raccoons and skunks seek partners too, and the beavers are pairing off. Owls sit on their eggs, and horned larks migrate. Flies appear in the sunny corners of the barn.

Then on the 18th day of the year's second month, the sun reaches a declination of 11 degrees, 53 minutes, the halfway point to equinox. The sun enters Pisces at the same time, and initiates the season of Early Spring, a six-week period of changeable conditions ,infiltrated ever so slowly by warmer and warmer temperatures that finally bring the first trees and the early bulbs to bloom.

By the 19th, moss will be growing a little more on the old logs, and crocus, daffodil and tulip foliage will have pushed out above the mulch. Garlic planted in late November will be at least six inches tall. The first rhubarb leaves will be unfolding. Henbit can be blossoming in the alleys, skunk cabbage in the swamps, aconites and snowdrops in a yard or two.

These soft days of Early Spring tell Canadian geese, mallards, canvasback ducks and killdeer to check out sites for laying eggs. Jenny wrens are making nests, and the milder afternoons call out the moths and water striders. Earthworms become active again; any day now, you will see them crossing roads and sidewalks in the lukewarm rains.

Ragwort and dock grow back in the swamps during Early Spring. A few deep red peony stalks appear underneath the mulch. Then more yellow aconite, white snow drops and yellow and purple snow crocus bloom. Pussy willows open wide.

Then, the last week of the month, as the Groundhog Moon wanes into its final quarter, along comes Snowdrop Winter Week, a time of meteorological ambivalence, promising hepatica, then backsliding.

First the warmth: The fifth major high pressure system of February comes through on the 20th, but it is typically the weakest front of the month, and highs reach above 50 (and sometimes even 60) three days in ten, and another five in ten are in the mild 40s.

And this week brings the first day since November 28th that the chances for highs just in the 20s or teens falls to almost zero!

Then a step backward: Snowdrop Winter arrives on the 24th, often one of the windiest days of the month, and colder temperatures often return for up to 72 hours. Snow or sleet falls almost half the time, but this is the last week of winter that chances for frozen precipitation climb so high.

On the 26th, Snowdrop Winter starts to recede, and from that day forward, average temperatures swell one degree every 72 hours (instead of every 24 to 36 hours) until the second week of June, and each day now brings some visible, measurable rise in the fortunes of spring.

By the time the Groundhog Day Thaw is over, the Sun will have climbed past a declination of 16 degrees, more than 30 percent of the way to spring equinox.

Daybook

1983: The first thunderstorm of the year, high near 50. Chipmunk seen running across the road. First robin seen at Wilberforce.

1984: Jacoby Swamp: Bees were out today, and the swamp streams were open in the thaw. One skunk cabbage had survived the cold. I saw one opossum that had been run over on Corry Street.

1986: Moss growing as logs warm in the longer days. A few peony knuckles, bleeding heart, rhubarb coming out of the mulch. Blue jay bobbing up and down, calling at 8:15 a.m. in the warm, 38-degree, misty morning. At Jacoby, seas of strong green cress. Robin heard. Ragwort growing.

1987: Cardinal heard 7:22 a.m. At Sycamore Hole, minnows biting, but no carp. Starlings, woodpeckers, bobwhite loud in the late afternoon. Winter abandoning its silence.

1992: On the way home from Fairborn last night, Jeanie smelled a skunk, first of the year

1993: Late Winter continues quiet; or maybe I've been inside more. But Jeanie's heard nothing either.

1997: When I was in the attic binding books at 7:35 a.m., a flock of geese flew over, close by my head, honking. Yesterday I saw two flocks crossing Dayton-Yellow Springs Road – and I saw a couple more flocks going over last week – activity is picking up for sure. Leaving for church about 10:50, I came out of the house into the cloudy, mild morning, into a chorus of cardinals, sparrows and starlings. They sang all the way down Dayton Street to St. Paul's. In the background, the first doves of the year. In the greenhouse, whiteflies getting worse in the tomatoes. Lettuce is doing well, though; I brought it in before the worst cold of December, and two heads have held their own, grown fat and squat sitting in their small four-inch pot. On the floor, the impatiens are becoming more tattered. I wonder if any will survive until May.

1999: Misty, soft morning, light rain, a little fog, barometer dropping. Iris in the pond has grown an inch or so in the past week.

2002: First cardinal at 7:13 a.m. Throughout the day, woodpeckers active. Insects are probably on the move.

2009: The thaw ended last night, and it's crisp this morning, but there's plenty of sun. We smelled a skunk on the way to Cedarville, and a cardinal was singing when we got back at about 11:00. One blue jay bell call heard at 9:00, and robins are peeping and chirping all around.

2012: Geese flew north of town, honking at 7:23 a.m., crows two minutes later, the earliest I've heard them this year. More sun and mild, a light northwest wind, the day warming into the 40s. Walking Bella this morning down the Stafford-Phillips Street alley, as I approached Limestone at 9:35, I heard a cardinal singing, and he sang while I walked west toward High, and then another cardinal started singing in the woods on the other side of High. Starlings are consistent visitors to the feeders this Late Winter, and this morning I saw them about in the alleys. This afternoon on the way out of town, Jeanie and passed a very substantial patch of full-blooming purple snow crocus on Dayton

Street. From Vermont, Cathy wrote that she saw somebody getting ready to tap the maple trees today, "very early for up here," she said.

2013: No Groundhog Day Thaw this year. Snow throughout the morning and afternoon, covering the budding aconites, but I saw sparrows dive into a rough mating clutch by the side of Limestone Street as I was driving to the shop.

2014: Icing on the roads and sidewalks from a rain-ice mix. After yesterday's melting, the back yard is mottled with snow and brown grasses, all of the Osage fruits akimbo, chewed and scattered by the squirrels and raccoons.

2015: Raw north wind today, sun and clouds, and one robin sitting, all fluffed and peeping, in the crab apple tree. Shulamit sent a photo of the same sight, could have been taken from my tree.

2016: Another soft morning: I walked out into the yard at 7:00 with Jill into robin calls, like from a small flock in the surrounding honeysuckles. Jill smelled a skunk by the Catholic church, but I could barely catch the odor. By 7:45, doves were calling all about, cardinals in the distance. To the west, a blizzard shuts down the Plains. A thunderstorm and hard rain this evening. I slept with the window open so I could listen to the rain.

2018: A fly emerged in the greenhouse this morning, even after last night's hard cold front and greenhouse temperature at 47 degrees. Ed Oxley reports that he has had snowdrops blooming for weeks. He has also seen huge flocks of geese passing over the river near his house, complementing the gathering and activity of geese near Ellis Pond. When I asked Casey and Mary Sue about the geese there, they talked about several hundred through the winter, but nothing like what is there now.

2019: Seventeen degrees and icing fog. The groundhog can't see his shadow in cover like that, but I heard the first cardinal at 7:26. As I walked Jill home at 10:00, crows were calling, cardinals singing steadily, sparrows chattering. Louise reported seeing two bluebirds in her yard, "the first ever there." Three medium-sized flocks of geese across from the pond, feeding in the melting snow.

2020: Almost 60 degrees this afternoon, the barometer plummeting, the Groundhog Day Thaw wind hard from the southwest, almost whitecaps on Ellis Pond This morning, I heard crows at 7:35, no cardinals. But all cardinals were active all around the yard, singing, along with titmice and chickadees at around 10:00. In the circle garden, daffodils are up an inch or two. The ditch lily bed shows a few shoots. In the front dooryard, snowdrops are up, the white tips showing on some of them. The buds of one Lenten rose are straining, losing their green.

Leslie and Bruce report thousands of starlings visiting their trees today, and the call of a grackle in the middle of starling chirping and whistling.

And from Reilly Dixon: "I saw a bald eagle flying Northwest, right over the intersection of E. Enon Rd. and Yellow Springs-Fairfield Rd. on Sunday, Feb. 2 at approximately 12:15 p.m. There was no mistaking it (with it's stark white head), but I sure couldn't believe it!"

Bit by bit, the sightings of bald eagles increase, adding to the natural history of the region.

2022: Stink bugs have emerged at Tat's house in Madison, Wisconsin, and at Jill's here in Yellow Springs. Today I saw other reports of folks in Yellow Springs finding those insects, too.

In February
All of a sudden there's a lot more light
And it's a warm light – snow melts off the roof,
The first lambs are born in the barn cellar,
The hens start laying, the mare comes into season,
And I notice that the geraniums at the window
Have pushed their stalks up eight inches
And covered them with brick-pink blossoms.

Kate Barnes

February 3rd
The 34th Day of the Year

So when you come to those dark February days of doubt, you go and listen to the maples, feel them, let their slow, impalpable pulse of soil and sun flow into you.... And you know that things are waking up down at the root of this tree. Sap is getting ready to work its way upward. You know, just as sure as you know what day it is.

Hal Borland

Sunrise/set: 7:42/5:55
Day's Length: 10 hours 13 minutes
Average High/Low: 35/19
Average Temperature: 27
Record High: 64 – 1890
Record Low: - 8 – 1902

Weather
The first high pressure system of the month often crosses the Mississippi on February 3rd, bringing much colder weather, with a 15 percent chance of below-zero temperatures for the first time since the 21st of January; this is just the beginning of a week-long period of increased possibilities for bitter morning lows. Today's temperature distribution: highs rise to the 50s fifteen percent of the years, into the 40s in 25 percent of the years, into the 30s in 35 percent, into the 20s or below 25 percent. Clouds are likely: today is one of the six February days on which there is just a 30 percent chance of sun. Precipitation: four times in a decade.

Natural Calendar
Signs are accumulating, spring a matter of quantity, number of sprouts, number of leaves and birds, landmark after landmark. Swept up by warm southwest winds, more robins and bluebirds reach the Great Lakes. Starlings whistle and chatter close to sunrise; the crows and cardinals and doves join in. Flies and bees look for skunk cabbage when temperatures warm to 50 degrees.

Berries from the hackberry trees have fallen to the snow,

leftovers from flocks of winter starlings. Stalks of astilbe, hosta, aster, Jerusalem artichokes are still erect, but their heads hang broken. Winterberry has dark olive-green-brown leaves, seeds holding. Black seeds of hosta lie across the snow. The last petals of oakleaf hydrangea and the rust brown seeds of the redbuds give way. In the Mid-Atlantic and the East, about 15 weeks remain before the most tender flowers and vegetables can be planted outdoors. Gardeners can put in hardier varieties in about eight weeks.

Daybook

1983: Second robin of the year seen at Wilberforce.

1987: Cardinal sang at 7:15 a.m.

1988: River flooding at the Glen after two days of rain.

1989: Huge Siberian cold wave preceding new moon, sent temperatures to -40 in Minnesota, but only down to normal here.

1990: Cardinal sang at 7:26 a.m.

1991: Jacoby Swamp: The first bee followed me through the watercress. Fat red skunk cabbage open in the streams.

1992: Jacoby Swamp: Sun and middle 50s. The woods quiet for most of the walk, one flicker, one bobwhite, one woodpecker heard. Juncos seen in the dense brush near the upper entry. Wild roses with a few new leaves, some chickweed. A clear blue to the sky, bright patches of green grass. Skunk cabbage sticking out in spots, maybe a finger-length high, skinny and dark from the frost.

1993: Sparrows chattering in the far trees at Wilberforce the past two mornings, a breakdown of the late-winter silence; cardinals at the bird feeder, still not singing. Snowdrops up an inch.

1995: January's cold has given way to thaw. Now with the snow gone, the land has been transformed. In some ways, nothing has changed with the arrival of the New Year. The trees are still bare,

and no new sprouts have appeared in the
undergrowth. Pussy willow catkins are thin and tight. Forsythia
buds show no hint of their February blush.

Autumn's fruits, however, are giving way to the weather,
measuring the advance of the Northern Hemisphere back toward
the sun. The hulls of last June's sweet rockets and August's wild
cucumbers are empty, brittle and delicate like shed snakeskin. The
Japanese knotweed leaves hang like huge russet cocoons.
Milkweed pods are stained and empty. The feathery tufts of
virgin's bower, soft and thick in late November, have blown away
in the wind. The final rose of Sharon seeds lie precariously in their
open calices. Worn seed heads of ironweed are half gone.

The dried flower clusters of purple coneflowers and
zinnias, tough and unyielding a month ago, crumble between my
fingers. Honeysuckle and euonymus berries still hang to their
branches, but their firmness is gone. Osage fruit is darkening
quickly, breaking down, squashy.

Taking my time, enjoying the warmth, I check the buds on
trees and shrubs: Hard, scarlet buds on the wild multiflora roses;
box elder buds, barely visible, tucked tightly to their green
branches; privet buds, minute and black; pale, supple buds of the
honeysuckle; on the blackberry canes were blood-red buds, their
color spreading to the sides of the stalks.

I feel the fleshy, orange buds of the buckeyes; the tight,
round, silver buds of the dogwoods, each one marking the tip of its
limb; the stiff, woody buds of the crab apples; the pale green buds
of the lilac; the sharp and thorn-like buds of the American beech;
the deep purple bud clusters of the red maples; the phallic
protrusions of the ginkgo.

I measure the gray velvety buds of the white magnolia; the
tiny russet linden buds; the yellow-brown, fat sweet gum buds
growing beside their dangling fruit; birch buds with their willowy
catkins; the buds of the tree-of-heaven, hiding in the hollows of
last year's branches; flushed azalea buds protected by their shining
leaves.

As the thaw deepens, remnants of the past year no longer
point to the warmth of last October. In the pond, wild iris spears
that braved weeks of ice stand strong around the broken strands of
lizard's tail. As the bamboo in my south garden recovers from the

weight of the snow, it shows sweet rockets, ground ivy, great mullein, celandine, wild lettuce, dock, sweet Williams and lamb's ear waiting for April and May.

1996: As I go through the daybook, it seems ridiculous to edit the signs of spring. Whether they are major signs or minor signs, it's their accumulation that really matters, whether they come in one year or in a series of years

1999: North along the bike path to the highway, maybe five miles: mild partly cloudy, haze, south wind. A flock of robins in a soybean field. Passed a small flock of juncos. Locust pods fallen on the path, another increment of spring.

2000: The Groundhog Day thaw was chilly this year, the temperatures softening into the 30s, but not really touching the foot of snow that has covered the ground for the past two weeks. After the sighting of robins in the crab apples at the end of January, no new bird observations at all, no cardinal songs, no blue jays or doves. A year ago, the crocus was in bloom.

2002: Doves called at 7:12 this morning, cardinals at 7:13.

2003: On the way to Washington Court House, I saw three opossums that had been killed on the roads last night in the thaw. At the mill, woodpeckers, cardinals, sparrows loud.

2006: Before the six-week thaw ended today, I found four pussy willow catkins emerging along the east fence.

2008: The weather has been about average these past few days, no movement to spring that I've been able to see. The mornings are still rather quiet, and only the appearance of finches and the starlings at the feeders suggesting change. In the alley, no birds, only a squirrel chattering today.

2009: A cardinal sang at 7:29 this morning, and as I walked Bella in the alley, more cardinals were singing; I heard a titmouse and chattering robins, too.

2010: Cardinals sing off and on through the day, but none heard before sunrise yet, even in the Groundhog Day Thaw. A large "V" of geese flew over the alley as I was walking Bella about 9:30 this morning.

2012: Coyotes howling west of town at 6:00 a.m. The aconite buds on Stafford Street are even larger and yellower and rounder this morning, but still not open. Henbit buds are pink along Limestone. I heard a cardinal singing along High Street as Bella and I were walking a little after 10:00, and then a dove called, the very first of the year. The national news reports azaleas flowering now in southern Georgia, about three to four weeks ahead of average.

2014: Several robins on the old schoolhouse lawn this afternoon. More sweet gum balls keep falling along Dayton Street.

2015: Crows at 7:33 a.m. Michelle wrote that the Flying Mouse Farm had tapped the maples today.

2016: The yard was flooded from last night's thunderstorm, and Ellis Pond and the rivers were high. A handful of snowdrops bloomed in the dooryard late this morning. In the circle garden and the west garden, squills and hyacinth stalks are two to three inches. In the pond, the larger fishes had started swimming around, breaking their winter stillness. Throughout the afternoon, the west wind blew hard, ending the thaw.

2017: Jane Scott wrote that when she went out to check the white tips of her snowdrops, she found some late-summer lily stalks had come under the mulch. "And it was a delight," she said, "to see a pair of red foxes courting behind our yard and snowdrops *blooming* in a Dayton Street yard."

2018: After a day working at the store, I drove by Ellis Pond to check on the geese. The thousands of honking birds that had filled the fields just a few days ago were gone. Far in the back toward Whitehall Farm, a small flock sat quietly. At a group of birders this morning, I asked about the geese, but no one had seen the mass gathering, even Dianne, who lived across the street from them.

2019: Deep thaw near 60 degrees, and the first cold front of the month is several days away, the pattern changed, perhaps, because of the movement of the polar vortex east. At Ellis Pond, hundreds of geese have spread out over a great portion of the fields. As Jill and I walked the path, we listened to them honking and screeching. On the way to Clifton, I saw about a dozen black buzzards working at a roadkill near the ditch.

2020: Karen called to report fireflies swarming on a neighbor's tree. Upon closer inspection, however, she found that the bark was glimmering in a laser light show! And Audrey Hackett wrote: "Winter aconite: I saw some in a yard at the corner of Dayton and Winter streets last Thursday. And yesterday, I saw some in my very own yard! Just three or four flowers, little gleams of yellow among the greening weeds. By my personal records, that's the earliest I've seen aconite here. What do your much deeper records say?" The earliest aconites I have recorded: Janet Hackett (no relation to Audrey) called on January 23, 1989 to report hers in bloom. During the early afternoon today, Ed Oxley called to say he had seen his first honeybee and his first aconite.

2022: The Groundhog Day Thaw has ended with a major storm from Texas through New England. Now at 5:00 p.m., heavy snow is falling here, is forecast to continue through the night. On the other hand, I saw a note in the paper that Ed Oxley's snowdrops were in full bloom along the Miami River.

Journal

When I was younger, I enjoyed fishing and the excitement of connection and of domination that accompanied it. When I was a boy, I killed the fish out of curiosity, and sometimes my mother would fry them for me. As an adult, when I killed and prepared and ate fish, I felt self-sufficient.

Now that I am old, I have a pond and four large koi. The fish have names: Buh buh (orange and white) and Bud (black and white), Princess (silver and black) and Golden Shark (gold and black). Last summer, they produced almost two-dozen fingerlings, kaleidoscopic in color.

Over the years, I have fallen in love with their ways: their caution and their eagerness, their loose hierarchies and their mutual support, their gentleness and their occasional spurts of excitement.

When the water warms above sixty degrees, they are active and swim freely. They come toward the edge of the pond when I approach with their food. They seem only mildly competitive, allowing the young to eat first if they choose.

In the winter, the cold seems to slow them all into contemplation. They move close to one another below the remnants of the lily pads. When I approach, they remain quiet, usually side-by-side, sometimes tucked together as though they were keeping each other warm. The fingerlings have a separate spot beside the lily roots, clustered like the adults in cenobitic security.

In this artificial sea, aerated by a pump and waterfall, climate controlled by a pond heater, the inhabitants lie out of danger, waiting for spring. Caring for them, I turn away from the violence of my youth and of my species. I pretend that all is well. I make believe that the peaceful community of winter fishes is the real world and that some benevolent caretaker watches over us all.

February 4th
The 35th Day of the Year

In the middle of winter, natural history reveals the growing power of spring. Like the steady rise of average temperatures, the accumulation of precedents through the years creates promise and potential for the fledgling season. In the concentric circles of February after February, the Earth's spin takes on a momentum in which every event has meaning for the same day every year.

Leon Quel

Sunrise/set: 7:41/5:57
Day's Length: 10 hours 16 minutes
Average High/Low: 35/19
Average Temperature: 27
Record High: 68 – 1890
Record Low: - 9 – 1912

Weather

Today is sunny 75 percent of the time, this being the brightest day in the first three weeks of February. Cold typically accompanies the clear skies: highs on February 4ths are in the teens five percent of the time, the 20s or 30s forty percent, the 40s thirty percent, the 50s fifteen percent and the 60s only ten percent. Chances of snow diminish somewhat from the first days of the month, dropping to 30 percent.

Natural Calendar

The pollen season, which ended with early winter, has now begun again across the South with the blooming of mountain cedar, acacia, smooth alder, bald cypress, American elm, red maple, white poplar and black willow. Bluegrass, which stopped flowering in midsummer, revives and starts its seeding cycle. As the February thaws bring moisture and warmth from the Gulf of Mexico, they also bring the pollen from all these flowers to the North. Tree pollen season peaks throughout the rest of the country in April and May. Grass pollen is most intense in May and June, weed and wildflower pollen in August through October.

1986: I found an Asian ladybeetle crawling on the plants in my office this afternoon. At the Covered Bridge, hemlock is about half a foot tall, moss growing, the river high. In the yard: a few peony spears, bleeding heart barely visible, some rhubarb two inches. Ground temperature at 40 degrees

1987: Cardinal singing at 7:16 a.m. South of Sycamore hole, I caught a small-mouthed bass at 5:00 this afternoon, the only one I've ever brought in there.

1989: Jeni reports cars covered with pollen in Jacksonville, Florida.

1991: Cardinals singing from the mid afternoon. First doves heard calling steadily between five and six o'clock this evening.

1993: This afternoon at Jacoby, sun and cool. Wingstem seeds still holding. In the swamp, beside the ice, skunk cabbage was in full bloom, plump, sleek, and flushed.

1998: A small flock of juncos seen near Wilberforce this noon.

1999: Crows at 7:25 a.m., dark, gray dawn, mild, barometer falling. Now the golden snow crocuses are in full bloom. Hyacinth leaves up. Daffodils and garlic three inches, the land ripening quickly.

2004: Ed Oxley calls from the Earth Rose store downtown, says he saw the first buzzard today west of town along Fairfield Pike.

2005: Casey called this afternoon: The overwintering flock of buzzards was on the wing, feathers shining in the sun.

2009: A cardinal was singing when I went outside this morning at 7:45. Along High Street, the bittersweet berries seem to be falling more now, the sidewalk covered with berries that must have fallen just this past week – since the walk was shoveled. This noon, a large flock of starlings settled in the south hackberry tree.

2010: Crows early but no cardinals heard until a little after 8:00 this morning – then, when the sun was maybe two or three fingers above the horizon, steady cardinal song. Tufted titmouse heard on Stafford Street. A snowstorm forecast for tomorrow, but there was frost on the car, and the barometer is holding high.

2011: A screech owl was calling when I went outside about 6:45 this morning. A cardinal sang at 7:15, and crows came through at 7:25. Blue jays whining after breakfast. The barometer has risen to 30.50, the storm having moved well to the east, but the sky is still overcast.

2013: When I walked Bella in the snow at 8:30 this morning, cardinal song accompanied us all the way around several blocks. In the alley, a flock of juncos, and crows passed overhead.

2014: Crows at 7:14 a.m., cardinals at 7:16, and the first dove heard, very faint over on Limestone Street at 7:22. Ed Oxley stopped by with pictures of his snowdrops way up out of the ground, white tips showing, each clump rising above the snow.

2016: As Jill and I walked down Elm Street this morning, we heard a song sparrow and a cardinal singing together at 7:15, on time in spite of wind and clouds. Asian lady beetles continue to appear and wander in Jill's kitchen. Cardinals and doves call throughout the morning, light snow falling.

2017: Clear and 10 degrees, down Limestone Street at 8:45 this morning, tufted titmouse singing steadily, house sparrows chattering, several cardinal calls, crows flying over. Audrey Hackett wrote from North High Street at 3:35: "A flock of eastern bluebirds appeared in our backyard this afternoon. Four males and at least one female (we were slower to identify the dun-colored females). They were gorgeous! They stayed quite a few minutes on the low branches of our redbuds, on our clothesline and on the neighbor's fence, flitting a bit among these but also perching quietly."

2018: Peter and Mary Sue wrote that they had seen a pair of Ross's geese in the with Canadian geese at Ellis Pond.

2019: Cardinals sang as I came outside at 7:17 this morning, sang throughout my walk with Ranger, my new border collie. Song sparrows and a red-bellied woodpecker started in about 7:30, crows about the same time. Woodpecker tapping off and on during the walk. One faint dove call heard a block away. As I was at Lauds about 9:00, I heard a robin peeping by the koi pond in the south garden. Snowdrops up, white tips showing, in the dooryard garden. In the warm afternoon, I counted between 300 to 400 geese all spread out on the fields across from Ellis Pond. Enoch's crew came by and cut up the hackberry tree that had fallen over the back yard two weeks ago, the yard pretty muddy from the rain and thaw and then the tramping around of the workers.

2020: The white-flowered hellebore opened all the way today in the last hours of the thaw, and Casey called to report he had seen a bluebird while he was walking his dog over near the college.

2021: Sleet, dropping barometer, deep cold forecast in a few days, grackles, blackbirds and cowbirds swarm the feeders in the afternoon. I read that Ed Oxley, who has kept me informed about the first snowdrop bloom for many years, died today. His flowers along the Miami River north of town were always the earliest, blossoming well before anything here in town.

2022: In the wake of yesterday's storm and six inches of snow, the first winter starling arrived at my window feeder. Jeff sent a photo of several doves in his tree, waiting to be fed.

2023: Casey sends a photo of budded snowdrops.

What light is tenderer
Than this of early February
At 5:05 p.m. or so,
Just trying brightness out?

John Updike

February 5th
The 36th Day of the Year

Paperwhites
slant, shift balance
in a shallow field.
Roots mass,
tendril uselessly
against the brittle
mother-shell.
Don't try to milk this breast:
tilt your mouth,
receive.

Liz Porter, "February, forced"

Sunrise/set: 7:40/5:58
Day's Length: 10 hours 18 minutes
Average High/Low: 36/19
Average Temperature: 27
Record High: 65 – 1927
Record Low: - 10 – 1886

Weather
Chances of highs in the 50s are 20 percent, of 40s ten percent, 30s thirty percent, of 20s thirty percent, of teens ten percent. Below-zero temperatures occur on 15 percent of the mornings. Rain occurs 25 percent of the time, snow another ten percent. Completely overcast conditions: 50 percent of the time. The barometer is often dropping on this date in anticipation of the second major high-pressure system of the month.

Natural Calendar
Even though the Groundhog Day Thaw is over, and history says these should be some of the coldest days of winter, crocus, daffodil and tulip foliage often emerges. Garlic planted in November has sometimes pushed out of the ground; cloves set in early October are already several inches high. Sometimes more than half of the pussy willows have opened. All along the 40th

Parallel, people are getting ready to tap maples for sap.

Daybook

1987: Cardinals singing by 7:15 a.m. Geese flew over at 8:10, doves call ten minutes later. Flies are out in the sunny 50-degree afternoon. First snowdrops reported up but not blooming. Some daffodils and tulips pushing up, too.

1991: First doves heard this morning about 7:15.

1993: Finally: cardinals at 7:10 a.m. outside the back door. At Wilberforce, doves and cardinals when I got to work around 7:45 a.m.

1994: This morning at 7:30, I could hear cardinals singing from all directions. They are setting their territories on every lot in the neighborhood. Still no doves.

1998: A few juncos today along the road southeast of town

2000: Skunk smell reported last night. And cardinal song heard this morning.

2002: Two long flocks of crows seen along the freeway just east of Springfield this morning. Skunk killed on the road to Xenia one or two nights ago.

2005: Cardinal songs steady now from a little before 7:00 a.m. Doves have joined in after sunrise.

2006: After snow and ice, two golden snow crocuses were opening under the bamboo in the south garden.

2008: Thunderstorm at 5:30 this morning and odor of a skunk. Hard rain throughout the area all day, considerable flooding. Tornadoes kill dozens in Tennessee and Arkansas in the middle of the night as a tremendous low crosses the country west to east.

2009: Inventory in the snow, in the afternoon before the thaw,

42

gibbous moon rising in the clear, robin's-egg blue sky: Six to ten inches of snow still left, now pocked with rabbit, dog and my own prints. Bamboo leaves grayed and shriveled by the cold January, some leaves shedding. Mexican sunflower heads white and withered, bending double. Ice around the pond waterfall, the heater helping the iris to grow back maybe three inches. Tight brown buds on the lilacs. Peeping of robins, passing of crows. Fragile pokeweed, berries gone, only stems left. Skirts of sunflower seed hulls left all around the bird feeders. Crab apples in the snow, the crab apple tree – like the hackberry – ravaged by the starlings a day ago. Rose leaves dark olive brown. Gray rosemary and butterfly bush stalks. One green sweet William showing through the ice. Yellowish Joe Pye heads, dun heads of monarda and stonecrop, pale iris spears , rose of Sharon pods half empty, open like hands to the sky.

2011: More snow today, but the crows were up at 7:19. I saw Peter yesterday, and he said the two overwintering sandhill cranes were still here.

2012: The first violet snow crocus in the east garden opened this morning in the sun, snowdrops beside it in full bloom. March in February.

2015: Pale, dawn-blue, clear sky, round moon setting, 8 degrees, barometer at 30.36, no wind, an inch of new snow on the ground: The first crows flew over from the northeast at 7:14. Then the first cardinals that I've heard before sunrise called at 7:15 from the Stafford Street alley. Finally, I hear the cycle in motion.

2016: Yesterday's blooming snowdrops all drooped and closed in this morning's frost.

2017: Mild 36 degrees and scattered clouds, only a slight breeze, Sunday morning, faint odor of skunk: I went out around the neighborhood at 7:15, first bird (song sparrow?) at 7:21, a house sparrow at 7:25, crows at 7:33, cardinal call notes in the backyard honeysuckles at 7:39, the first dove at 7:41, a distant male cardinal at 7:42. As I walked, I saw the sun shining on contrails, soft gold above the dawn. This afternoon in the garden, a few white pussy willows bright against the deep blue sky.

2018: I watched a Savannah sparrow and a dark-eyed junco rooting in the leaves by the north trellis this afternoon.

2021: Chris writes: "We seem to have some very busy Carolina wrens this week. One or more of them have been exploring the eaves of the outbuilding, the shroud of the oven vent, windowsills, pecking at windows . . . . Several years ago I had a Carolina wren in our woodshed and it refused to come out. That was right before a severe cold snap. I wonder if they know cold is coming, and start looking for shelter. I would gladly offer our cabin, but I doubt the wren would find it (or the cat) hospitable!"

Journal
Pangur, white Pangur,
How happy we are
alone together, Scholar and cat,
Each has his own work to do daily,
For you it is hunting,
For me study.
Your shining eye
Watches the wall; my feeble eye
Is fixed on a book.

"White Pangur," translated by W.H. Auden

This winter I had planned to begin the new year at the start of Advent, December 3. I intended to close the door on autumn, but I failed to make ceremony out of the end of the cycle, unable to come to closure in the ways the religious people do, and the ways my upbringing dictated. The older rituals I had practiced no longer held up, and I even fled from them, surprised at my feelings, unable to socialize the start of the season.

But a friend of mine sent me the "Hermit Songs" of anonymous Irish monks and scholars who, a thousand years ago, scribbled their verses in the margins of the manuscripts they were copying. The songs made sense to me just at the right time, especially the one about white Pangur. They invited me to enter the colder time of year in a different way, reminded me that I could embrace these hermetic fragments instead of the formal, organized piety, awash in implications and sentiments, with which I was already overburdened.

So I linger now within the monkish, medieval mood of these poems, happy to adopt their spirit and enter into the isolation of winter with the cats I have, hunkering down into January withdrawal. And I sit and write these notes with the family cat named Monk lying across my forearms; I embrace the contentment of the ancient cleric:

Thus we live ever
Without tedium or envy.
Pangur, white Pangur,
How happy we are.

The Irish author, without hymn or litany, found his peace in what I imagine to have been a stark and lonely habitat, warmed only by a fireplace. Within the context of his song, the true cenobitic community is not one of fellow monks, is not validated by formal liturgy or by magical meals of remembrance, but is rather a community of lone workers and seekers. The cell of winter and the companionship possessed there are rare gifts of seclusion and contemplation, gifts of the silent journeying into reflection or study, rewards of the waiting in friendship with Pangur for an elusive prize, without a sense of tedium or envy, happy, from inside the shelter of shared myopia

The sand and the sea and the raindrops,
and the days of eternity, who can assess them?
The height of the sky and the breadth of the earth,
and the depth of the abyss, who can probe them?

Ecclesiasticus

February 6th
The 37th Day of the Year

Now every motion of the day
presents another portion of the Spring,
the calling of the cardinal and the jay,
the robin's whinny, juncos on the wing.

Robert Ames

Sunrise/set: 7:39/5:59
Day's Length: 10 hours 20 minutes
Average High/Low: 36/19
Average Temperature: 28
Record High: 61 – 1925 (60 – 2017)
Record Low: - 8 – 1977

Weather

Odds in favor of cold continue strong as the second high-pressure system of the month arrives. More below-zero temperatures are recorded for this date than for any other February day in my record. Highs in the 50s, however, do come 15 percent of the years, 40s another 15 percent, with chillier 30s recorded 30 percent of the time, 20s twenty percent of the time, teens ten percent, and single digits five percent. Overcast conditions occur five days in ten on this date. Rain falls ten percent of the days, snow 35 percent.

Natural Calendar

On this date, the day's length is a full hour longer than it was on December 26th all along the 40th Parallel.

Daybook

1983: I feel the isolation of winter testing me, the long spells without sun, the monotony of landscape without change.

1984: Another dead opossum on Grinnell Road this morning. Even in this cold winter, just one warm spell brought the possums out.

1986: First thunderstorm of the year.

1992: Cardinals strong and steady by 8:00 a.m.

1993: First blue jay seen staking out territory down toward Stafford Street. Cardinals sing off and on all day, doves too. Loud sparrow chatter, long through the morning.

1998: Along the back roads, one skunk killed overnight. Three flocks of juncos seen within a mile or so. The great movement is underway.

2004: Beth Bridgeman called to say her Chinese witch hazel had been blooming all week. I called the nursery she bought it from. The owner, Craig Jaynes, said that most of his *Hamamelis* (witch hazels) were flowering. He added that hellebores were blossoming in the greenhouse now, too. At home, our hellebores have buds.

2005: At about 10:00 p.m., I stood and listened to a screech owl whinnying in the back trees.

2008: More rain today, more flooding. A gray, damp, chilly day: Ohio February. In the front garden and in Don's yard, snowdrops are up an inch, white buds showing. Under the Osage tree in the back yard, Osage fruits are mostly purple-brown, and squirrels or raccoons tear them apart. One opossum seen dead on the Grinnell road last night. Still no doves heard at all. Three starlings in Don's black walnut tree at about 10:00 this morning.

2009: Cardinal heard when I went outside at 7:40 this morning. Steady south wind but still cold at 10:00. The first of the thaw finally arrived this afternoon, highs finally into the 40s. Sun all day and warm through the night.

2010: Eight inches of snow fell yesterday and this morning as the Groundhog Day Thaw ended with cold and wind. Today, the bird feeders were crowded with all kinds of songbirds and a substantial flock of starlings – the most starlings that have fed here all winter. Crows called in the morning, but no cardinals or doves heard.

2011: Crows at 7:19 again this morning, and when I went outside to feed the birds a little after sunrise, cardinals were in full song, and crows continued to fly over the yard. More starlings at the feeder again today.

2012: Robin peeping before dawn when I went out to feed the sparrows and cardinals.

2013: Crows at 7:20 this morning, first cardinal heard at 7:50.

2015: Crows at 7:20 this morning,

2016: Clear, frost, rising crescent moon just north of Venus: First cardinal at 7:08, first song sparrow at 7:11, crows by 7:20. Kate Mooneyham sent a photo of violet crocus opening in front of the Emporium today. This evening at 9:45, skunk odor along Dayton-Yellow Springs road when Jill and I were coming back from Beavercreek.

2017: Ed Oxley wrote today that when he was out in the garden today at around 4:00 p.m., he saw "all of a half dozen to a dozen honeybees visiting my snowdrops. I thought that was a great sign, so I looked around the yard and found eight early crocus blooming. So spring is on the way. Live is coming back to the Miami Valley."
    Coming home from a long walk with Jill (on which I saw a bluebird flock) in 55-degree hazy weather, I found one of the deep red hellebore flowers had undone its petals. A strong storm through the night, great claps of thunder and heavy rain.

2019: A ladybug on my sleeve this morning (like on the 7th in 1984). Mild in the 50s and heavy rain much of the day (almost two inches). The lower sections of the yard and the back patio are under water. In the dooryard garden, one snowdrop has budded, bud drooping down to flower. In the circle garden, spears of hyacinths and daffodils are up an inch or so. At the fields near Ellis Pond, hundreds of geese remain, and they are enjoying the flooded areas. And Chris Walker wrote to say he has been hearing Great

Horned Owls calling back and forth. Mating time. Chris also told me he had seen a flock of about 30 sandhill cranes flying south over his land this past week.

2020: Walking at 7:30, I heard a cardinal in the distance, then geese, then crows, then a chickadee making its "hey sweetie" mating call throughout the alley.

2022: The fields of snow near Ellis Pond are full of geese, at least 500, based on earlier counts.

2023: Now the open water at Ellis Pond is covered with geese, maybe 300, 400 or the possible 500 of last year. The gathering is reaching its peak. At the Glass Farm wetland, Jill and I thought we heard a few red-winged blackbird calls.

Journal

This past Friday, Buttercup the family bulldog and I were walking along the river into Mint Hollow. It was a rainy and windy afternoon, full of the scent of the thawing ground. I was thinking, while I walked, about spring, and about Lent, and Easter coming, and then about childhood Irish Catholic fasting and abstinence this time of year, of small change given up for "pagan babies" in distant lands, rosaries said after supper, the family praying for world peace, and for distant uncles and aunts, for all the war dead, for the Pope, and for secret intentions.

Those were Wisconsin Lents, with no possibility of a thaw until late March, darker afternoons than these, the ground covered with snow at least until Easter. When that feast finally arrived, even though the cold stayed, the wind came from the south more often, and the ice on puddles gave way easily to my rubber boots.

I practiced the Church year ritual until my early twenties. Then I left that structure behind for a complex of reasons, which included disagreements over dogma, rubric, liturgy, and policy. I became embarrassed by the clericalism, the jargon, the exclusivity, and the bad taste of formal Catholic practice. I took up instead something of Bertrand Russell's philosophy expressed so exquisitely in "A Free Man's Worship."

In Russell's vision of humanity cut off from the eternal, I found a brave defiance against death, and a noble alternative to an intrusive Church. I still have my copy of his essay, well worn. One of the more pointed passages I underlined in the early 1960s: "Brief and powerless is man's life; on him and all his race the slow, sure doom falls pitiless and dark. Blind to good and evil, reckless of destruction, omnipotent matter rolls on its relentless way; for man, condemned today to lose his dearest, tomorrow himself to pass through the gate of darkness, it remains only to cherish, ere yet the blow fall, the lofty thoughts that ennoble his little day."

Here to me was the ultimate self-sufficiency: the freedom from God, the freedom to define myself by my own grace, not His. Having been tyrannized so long by fear and guilt, I embraced Russell's gallant earthly heaven, and I tried to become his heroic human who, having given up vain hopes of a demeaning paradise, worshipped "at the shrine that his own hands have built, undismayed by the empire of chance."

Against the powerful common sense of Russell's position, however, against his careful arguments, and the majesty of his ideal, my childhood rhythms have returned to assert themselves. In spite of the absurdity of Catholicism, in spite of all my disagreements with it, I find myself carefully tracking its old seasons with my outdated missal. I say the rosary now, and I invoke the saints the way my mother taught me.

'It is not a social religion that I have, not anything I can pass on or down to anyone. It seems rather the triumph of emotion and illogic, the victory of an unshakable habit, possibly even of faith, over transitory reason. It seems to be the emergence of a hybrid, fifty-something spiritual madness, a blind and unexpected blend of my past and present, a new assertion of who I am becoming, free of institutional and Biblical preconceptions, free from Russell's compelling but bleak atheism.

The rain turned to sleet in Mint Hollow, and then there was thunder, the first I'd heard all year. The wind came up, and then snow started to fall in flakes so huge and so thick they hid the river.

Buttercup jumped at the noise, and her ears went back. She looked frightened, ran to me, scooted off up the path, then zoomed back, confused and nervous. I knelt down and held her to me, stroked her head and rubbed her back. I told her what she heard was neither the reproach of a wrathful Irish God nor the ghastly roar of Bertrand Russell's fatal and indifferent universe. It was instead, I reassured her, the first wild and mighty call of the rising Christ of Spring. Before sundown, I began the trimming of shrubs on the east end of the garden to open up the sky for summer growth.

On frosty mornings, song sparrows were the first to start, their songs tinkling and diffident. As dawn light turned the old fields a pale cream color, tufted titmice cried "Peedle-peedle-peedle!"; cardinals whistled "Wheet! Wheet! Wheet! Wheet!"; a few overwintering field sparrows opened their pink bills and trilled "Pew! Pew! Pew! Pewpewpew-pewpew!" In the woods bluejays made a peculiar ringing sound: "Tlapit! Tlapit!"

David Rains Wallace, *Idle Weeds*

February 7th
The 38th Day of the Year

There had been other signs of the turn of the seasons: the faint odor of skunk in the air…. And the stench of the cattail marsh….. It was a smell like the aroma of the skunk; overpoweringly sweet, penetrating and impossible to get rid of. And then in the distance could be heard the sound of a flock of blackbirds arriving, a rustling sound like the wind in the leaves of the cottonwood

Paul Gruchow, *Journal of a Prairie Year*

Sunrise/set: 7:38/6:00
Day's Length: 10 hours 22 minutes
Average High/Low: 36/20
Average Temperature: 28
Record High: 63 – 1925 (60 – 2017)
Record Low: - 8 – 1905

Weather
Continued cold is the rule. Highs reach above 50 ten percent of the time, 40s occur 20 percent, 30s thirty-five percent, 20s thirty percent, teens five percent. February 7th has just a 35 percent chance of rain or snow. The sun appears on more than half of the days.

Natural Calendar
Owlets and young bald eagles grow inside their eggs. Riding the warming winds, red-winged blackbirds, meadowlarks, starlings, cedar waxwings, snow buntings, and ducks of all kinds migrate, increasing the mass and power of spring.

Daybook
1984: I found a ladybug crawling around on one of my potted tomatoes today.

1990: This morning at 7:30, robins, doves and cardinals were singing. Background chatter of sparrows. Spring is growing louder every day. Dandelions at Wilberforce nearly open. Patches of chickweed flowering in the outside planter near the library.

1991: Crows active at night in south Springfield, roosting in the trees near the high school there.

1993: Cardinal sings 7:12 a.m. for the second morning in a row. When I was working outside cutting up the box elder, blue jays, cardinals and doves flew back and forth calling, sparrows chirping in the background. Sap from the tree was wet and running. In the garden, one rhubarb leaf has emerged.

1998: Doves heard this morning at 7:28. Then a cardinal, crows, titmouse. By 10:00 a.m., strong chorus. The sun shining, back yard covered with a layer of snow and ice starting to melt.

2001: On the way to Clifton this morning, I saw spring roadkills: an opossum, a groundhog and a skunk.

2008: Cardinal singing steadily when I came outside at 7:20 this morning. Finches feed daily now at the sack feeders.

2009: Before the thaw arrived last week, six to ten inches of snow were still left, pocked with rabbit tracks, dog tracks and my own footprints. The pussy willow buds were brown and tight. Hackberries and crab apples and small branches lay on top of the snow, leftovers from the starling flock that had come through the previous day.

On January 31st, the wind came straight from the south, chilly at midmorning but mild by the middle of the afternoon, highs finally rising into the 40s. The sun was bright through the day, and the wind blew all night, shifting to the southwest. On the morning of the 1st, cardinals were singing by 7:30. The snow was stubborn but was ceding to the wind. I could walk most of the alley on bare ground, and the oases of open earth were broadening under the trellis and bird feeders and around the sweet Williams and the iris.

The sun disappeared late in the morning, but the thaw did not let up, temperature climbing above 50. The south edge of the circle garden showed thyme and fresh deadnettle leaves. Rick

Donahoe wrote that noon to say he had seen buzzards, "three or four on a deer carcass out across from Stutzman's," and that John Whitmore had seen an ovenbird in the Glen (the ovenbird sighting especially interesting since April is usually the earliest they are seen in the area).

The wind held steady through the night, the patches of ground becoming much more prominent, some green showing in the grass, color coming back into the bamboo leaves in the Stafford Street alley.

A cardinal in the back woodlot sang at 7:12 this morning, crows right behind him. Starlings were all around downtown when I went to get the newspaper at 8:30. Out in the country, the morning horizon was hazy with spring. The roadsides and pastures were almost free of snow, but the wooded areas held on to their cold.

At South Glen in the afternoon at 4:00, temperature of 45 degrees, the sky robin's egg blue, I listened to crows and peeping robins and a pileated woodpecker. The frozen river had softened to decaying floes shifting away from shore, still held by the curve of the banks. Under the trees, the melting had revealed thousands of box elder seeds, pale dun like a new hatch of winged insects.

The path west into the low sun had lost its hard slickness, was slushy and easy to walk. Edges between spring and winter were everywhere, the landscape lying out like the variegated hide of Thoreau's leopard-earth. Extensive holes in the cover had opened around scattered tree trunks and plants, showing clumps of oak leaves, chickweed and sweet rocket, ragwort and great mullein, innumerable honeysuckle berries. By the time I got home, dozens of pussy willows were opening along the sidewalk, and the moon was coming up full over High Street.

2010: More starlings at the bird feeders now. Scotty reported half a dozen robins in snow-covered berry bushes. He said that he took photos of them gobbling berries.

2011: Light snow and the barometer falling in advance of a cold wave due tonight. Crows near 7:25 this morning, cardinals singing throughout the back woods before 8:00. Tat received a report from one of her friends in Madison, Wisconsin that she had seen two robins in her back yard on the 6th.

2013: The sun is warm and the day is clear, the snow melting around the snowdrops, which are all standing so tall now. Juncos still feeding along the northwest garden. And Michele from Flying Mouse Farm just let me know that they were starting to tap the trees today, the same day as in 2008 and 2009.

2014: Snow cover is up to a foot in many yards. At almost exactly 6:00 this evening, I went out to get wood and heard a screech owl's eerie descending call back in the neighbor's trees.

2015: Walking Bella this morning around 9:30, I heard cardinals up and down the neighborhood. A thaw coming today, rain tomorrow, highs in the middle and upper 40s. Michele from Flying Mouse Farm said they tapped the maples on the 4th and that the sap was running today.

2017: Another warm day throughout the Lower Midwest. From Keosauqua, Iowa (southeastern Iowa along the 40th Parallel), Rusty wrote: "We already have bluebirds looking for nests and checking out boxes." In my pond, the koi swim around slowly, but they are interested in me when I come close. The thermometer in the water reads 48 degrees.

2020: Light snow and cold, a cardinal at 7:32 this morning, a chickadee's two note "sweetee" call in the alley as I turned on to Limestone Street.

2023: Some daffodils six inches high, one found with a pubescent bud. More tree trimming in 50-degree weather.

Journal

In the long cold of the last few weeks, I have withdrawn into a fetal, psychic hibernation, reminiscing about childhood and about other retreats I have made from the weather and the world. This morning, while I was working alone in my attic bindery, listening to the wind and watching the snow, a memory mood from my hermetic high school years at Holy Cross Seminary came back and settled around me.

In my mind, I went back to the seminary crypt under the main chapel, a windowless basement of gray stone, with low ceilings and heavy pillars and pointed arches. It smelled like incense and beeswax. Slab altars lined the walls. The staff of priests, with the students as servers, said daily mass there.

I remembered the sense of complete protection I felt in that place, not only from the northern winter, but from conflicts with peers, hormonal temptations, adolescent ennui. Enveloped in that subterranean chamber and in its ritual, I was the wide-eyed adept. That dim, consecrated cave was the center of my practice, the passageway to the Path. The holy sacrifice which I attended was the ultimate act. The Latin exchange between server and celebrant was the great secret dialogue, the true code, communion with the living and the dead.

Outside the seminary, in the lonely, secular and snow-covered hills above the frozen river, away from sure and scented dogma and hierarchy, there was no salvation. But in the crypt I was safe; I belonged as I have never belonged since. Had I chosen, I could have stayed there forever; I had been born to the elect, and the magical words I witnessed and abetted could change common bread and wine into God.

Then one year, spring came to me while I prayed, and my devotion thawed, and what had once seemed so frightening and alien in winter flowered and sang. My vestments became too tight. Heaven lost its allure. I no longer wanted to be safe or to belong. The hills were green in the sun, and I longed only for the open river and for the magic of earth.

You are your own sky
With suns and stars and moons and winds
Enough to prophesy.

Celtus

February 8th
The 39th Day of the Year

*During February's brief thaw come gentle days when we gather
pussy willow sprays and dream of the green season.*

Gladys Tabor

Sunrise/set: 7:37/6:01
Day's Length: 10 hours 24 minutes
Average High/Low: 36/20
Average Temperature: 28
Record High: 69 – 1925
Record Low: - 6 – 1977

Weather
Today's high temperature distribution: five percent of the
days are in the 60s or 50s; forties come ten percent of the time, 30s
thirty percent, 20s forty percent, teens fifteen percent.   There is a
15 percent chance of a morning below zero. Rain almost never
falls on February 8th, and snow comes only one year in four. The
sky is completely overcast five days in ten on this date.

The Week Ahead
The second quarter of February is typically chilly, with
temperatures in the 30s or below occurring better than 60 percent
of the time. The likelihood of below-zero temperatures falls to half
of that of last week, however. The 11th ushers in the third major
cold wave of the month, and this is typically the last severe front of
winter. By the 14th, chances of highs in the 20s or below fall to
only ten percent, and by the 15th, chances of spring warmth above
50 degrees jump to 40 percent - the highest so far this year. This
change is so dramatic on regional weather charts, that it can easily
be called the beginning of Early Spring - a six-week period of
changeable conditions during which milder weather gradually
overwhelms the cold. Precipitation is generally light between the
7th and the 10th. Between the 11th and the 15th, however, each
day carries about a 50 percent chance of rain or snow.

Christian Richardt

The brighter afternoons of Late Winter give impetus to Groundhog, Opossum, Raccoon and Beaver Mating Seasons all across the nation. In Arkansas, Rhubarb Leafing Season coincides with Henbit Blooming Season in Lexington, Kentucky. Throughout the southern and central states, people are tapping trees in Maple Sap Season as Steelhead and Walleye Fishing Seasons gradually unfold in the Great Lakes. For gardeners in the Lower Midwest, these are sometimes the initial days of Onion Set Season; if the month is cold, onion eaters often wait until they see the red tips of peonies coming up at the beginning of Peony Growing Season.

The Stars

The Great Square will be setting in the west before midnight during February's second week. Perseus follows Cassiopeia into the northwest. Spring's Regulus will be well up in the sky on the other side of the horizon in the constellation Leo. Early summer's planting guide, Arcturus, is visible just before midnight in the northeast on February 12th. Libra lies due south along the horizon. Above it, the stars of Serpens lead toward the Corona Borealis, a formation that looks like a stellar necklace. In the far west, Regulus is the brightest star. In the east, the Vega is the brightest.

Daybook

1984: The first fly emerged in the greenhouse today. Or did he get in from outside?

1985: One bluebird seen crossing Wilberforce-Clifton Road. Cardinals singing well into the afternoon. A cabbage butterfly hatched in the greenhouse today. The temperature was hot inside from the sun, but 23 degrees outside.

1987: A fly in the greenhouse this afternoon.

1988: Nine robins in my gingko tree at 5:00 p.m. Snow on the ground, temperatures at 25 degrees.

1989: The sun is rising at an azimuth of 110 degrees, east-southeast, between the Danielson's pine trees and the northeast corner of their house. It sets at 255 degrees, to the right of the garage.

1990: Cardinals and doves at 7:10 a.m.

1991: Very first peony stalks are up, two red tips. Janet Hackett calls: her aconites are blooming.

1992: First tulips (three) are up along the rose fence.

1998: Cardinals singing at 7:10 a.m. As I walked to church at 8:30, sparrows were in full chorus, and a blue jay was chattering in the high pines. On the way downtown along Elm Street: five purple snow crocuses fully open in the sun. On Xenia Avenue, the first wasp of the year investigating the warm bricks on the south wall of Deaton's Hardware. A fat black fly sat on the community bulletin board.

1999: Crows at 7:14 a.m., cardinal at 7:16, cloudy and cold.

2006: I could smell a skunk in the back yard this morning, the second time there has been a skunk around this month.

2008: No cardinals until after sunrise this morning, still no dove calls this year. Around the yard, more crocus foliage is coming up, and what looks like the tips of hyacinths. Snowdrops have grown an inch in the past few days – in spite of or maybe because of the hard rains and flooding. Four doves (instead of starlings) in Don's tree this morning.

2009: The thaw continued through the night, three-fourths of the sidewalk now clear of ice, the patches of ground much more prominent, the brown space beginning to match the snow space, some green showing in the grass, color coming back into the bamboo leaves. A cardinal sang at 7:12 this morning, crows right behind him. Starlings were all around downtown when I went out to get the newspaper at 8:30. To Columbus late morning, the horizon hazy with spring. The roadsides and pastures almost free of snow, but the wooded areas hold on to their cold, and melting is much less. Snowmelt runoff in the ditches. Two flocks of crows seen but no starlings.

To South Glen in the afternoon at 4:00, 45 degrees: Sky robin's egg blue again. Crows and peeping robins and one pileated woodpecker heard. The river ice softened to floes shifting away from shore, still held by the curve of the banks. A few small clumps of ice and snow move by quickly on the high, dark river. Under the trees, thousands of box elder seeds unveiled by the snowmelt, pale dun like a hatch of new, winged insects. The path west had lost its hard slickness, was slushy and easy to walk on.

Everywhere there were edges between thaw and winter, the landscape lying out like the variegated hide of Thoreau's leopard-earth. Holes in the cover had opened around scattered tree trunks and plants, showing clumps of crisp oak leaves. Only fragments of green foliage revealed by the thaw, a few chickweed and sweet rocket, ragwort and great mullein, innumerable honeysuckle berries among them. The moss on old logs was still matted to the bark, in spite of days of warmth. At home, dozens of pussy willows were opening. I walked Bella about 9:30 this evening, the full moon high, the air crisp.

2010: Clear deep blue sky this morning, shining snow on shrubs and trees, the first below-zero reading of the winter, a minus 1. More starlings at the feeders.

2011: Light snow overnight, the sidewalk covered with a half an inch. Crows were passing through when I went outside at 7:10 this morning.

2012: A cardinal was singing in the Stafford Street alley as I walked Bella about 9:45 this morning.

2014: This morning when I was putting out birdseed I noticed that the bamboo leaves had all turned brown from the deep cold. This evening near eight o'clock, barometer dropping, snow coming, the screech owl's ghostly whinny in the back trees.

2015: Mild dawn in the 40s at the end of an out-of-sync thaw. Cardinals singing passim throughout the morning. Tiny yellow buds of aconites peer through the mulch along Stafford Street. Liz's snowdrops are a little ahead of mine, their white tips starting to bend. A high close to 60 in the afternoon.

2016: After the rain at 7:45, snow still coming from the west. Birdsong is common now: cardinals, crows, song sparrows, nuthatches, sparrows, robins.

2020: I saw the first starling at the feeder today. Leslie reports the first dove call.

2023: No doves heard so far, but temperatures have been well above normal. Daffodils are growing quickly, and the first pale green hellebores have opened in the dooryard. Under Janet's redbud, a stray violet snow crocus has bloomed. I continued to prune around the garden, but the weather has been so warm, I am too late to avoid stepping on new sprouts. Geese flew the yard over after dark.

Journal

A large black fly has emerged in the greenhouse during these first days of February, and it proceeds to explore the rest of our home, partial to the kitchen and the bathroom.

The family rightly wants the creature dispatched or at least relegated to the out-of-doors. But I am uneasy about killing a harbinger of spring, and the firstborn – under this roof – of the New Year.

So far the winter had been gentle; the fly must know what she is doing; she probably forecasts more by her surprise appearance than I could ever calculate with my charts. I am therefore remiss in my duty to get rid of the visitor. Maybe she will just go away, I say.

But as I sit in the greenhouse, typing my newspaper column two hours before sunrise, the fly is not only still here, she has become quite friendly, has taken a liking to me and to my colorful computer screen. She keeps reminding me of my duty to protect her, and of the dire meteorological and personal consequences of any aggression.

She zooms back and forth from my desk to the lamps in two other parts of the room, enjoys the air around the warm wood stove, returns after a few minutes to check up on me. Then she goes off to explore the geraniums, maybe observing the perennial aphids, maybe spying the one or two camelback crickets that have found sanctuary among the flowerpots.

Sometimes she's quiet. Once in a while she buzzes. At the moment, she doesn't seem interested in contaminating food or spreading germs. She's both coy and obtrusive, elusive and forward. It would be unthinkable that she had nothing to tell me. It is early in the morning, and we are alone. There is no one to see us together. Momentarily free from social expectations and responsibility, I can embrace the first fly of the year without remorse or guilt, smile at her attention, identify with her excitement at being alive in the artificial summer of my tomato and pepper plants, listen for her secret message.

Each day creates a subseason that shapes vision and emotion. Inter-seasonal days can offer more complex mixtures of change and stasis than those that lie in middle seasons; they also offer unexpected sanctuary, benign empty space between galaxies of leaves and buds and snow.

Bradford Townsend

February 9th
The 40th Day of the Year

It was how we knew winter would die.... In the dark of the barn night when it was still cold enough outside to make things break, in the warm dark night of the closed barn they came, and when we would open the door in the morning to start chores we could smell them, the new calves.

Gary Paulsen

Sunrise/set: 7:36/6:03
Day's Length: 10 hours 27 minutes
Average High/Low: 36/20
Average Temperature: 28
Record High: 63 – 1938, 65 – 2023
Record Low: - 21 – 1899

Weather
Temperature statistics for today: chances of highs in the teens are 15 percent; of 20s twenty-five percent; of 30s forty percent, of 40s five percent, and for fifties 10 percent, 60s five percent. Today is one of two days in the first 14 days of February on which chances of highs in the 50s are so great. Rain or snow comes 30 percent of the time, and the sun appears five times in a decade. The possibility of below-zero temperature continues at 15 percent.

Natural Calendar
February's warmest days reveal the most responsive places in the yard, areas of greener grass and the first flowers. "I think there are different climates even in one garden," said Evadine, who used to live down the street from me. "Some spots catch more sun, especially early in the year. Rocks and walls hold can hold heat for a few extra hours." The wind can spoil those sunny corners, she thought. "The right protection is necessary, too; mulch is so important now."

1983: First groundhog seen by the roadside. At the Covered Bridge, dock leaves are burned from the cold, but new foliage is poised, ready to replace the old.

1991: Five red-tailed hawks seen on the trip to Switzerland County in southern Indiana.

1992: North to Madison, Wisconsin: Red-tailed hawks common on the high wires.

1993: Temperature in the 50s today. First fly seen in my building at school. At home, when I was chopping wood in the back yard this afternoon, a sluggish housefly crawled up on my log.

2001: Daffodils emerging, some spears up half an inch.

2002: Cardinals sing at 7:04 a.m., crows follow three minutes later, the sky clear, temperature right at freezing. Daffodils are up three to four inches now, many buds visible. This afternoon, under a high near 60, a broad patch of purple and gold snow crocuses was blooming in the sun by the south wall. Crane flies were spinning in the sun north of the apple tree. As I weeded, small, black wolf spiders jumped through the dead grasses to escape my hands. When I checked for termites in the siding, I uncovered a cluster of ladybugs. Most of them remained huddled together as I worked around them. In the pond, algae is growing thicker from all the sun and mild afternoons. On my trip to Dayton and back, several opossum roadkills seen.

2006: Walking Bella this morning, I noticed all kinds of bittersweet berries fallen to the sidewalk. Had it happened overnight?

2009: Full moon setting hazy through the woods this morning, dusky horizon, soft air. Cardinal at 7:08 this morning. South wind continues. Bittersweet berries continuing their collapse. Snowdrops an inch high were uncovered overnight by the melting snow. The south wind kept blowing, the high reaching into the 50s again, snow disappearing more quickly, revealing foliage of lungwort and Lenten roses. The patches of bare earth that were encroaching on the snow yesterday have overrun much of the town. The triangle park is almost completely open now, and the walks are free of ice for the first time in weeks. I was able to get up to the roof to check the chimney, and as I came down, two long flocks of Canadian geese flew north low over the house, honking.

2010: Another snowstorm, this one bringing at least four to six inches on top of the eight the other day. At the feeders, a junco, two doves, a flock of starlings and lots of sparrows. As I was cleaning off the cars, I heard a robin and a red-winged blackbird.

2011: Crows at 7:25 this morning, very cold.

2012: Cardinals calling along High and Stafford Streets this morning around 10:15, but no pre-dawn songs heard yet.

2013: A cardinal sang loud and long at 7:05 this morning, the eastern sky dark orange. Crows joined at 7:17. When I went out to the truck, I smelled the first skunk of the year. I saw a pair of robins at the St. Clare Monastery just north of Cincinnati.

Then Liz wrote: "I spied a small flock of bluebirds at Ellis this morning— five or six I think! What a beautiful day it is. Spring is in the air."

I have lived in Yellow Springs for thirty-five years, and I have taken thousands of notes on different events in nature here, but I find that it is the notes about the seasons from family and friends (like Liz) and acquaintances and readers that mean the most to me.

This web of persons and events and years informs a different kind of season than I first suspected might exist. I used to think of spring as a private revelation, and I delighted in seeing it accumulate year after year in repetition and variation. Then a community voice came to what I saw, extending my reach and also teaching me. And I am learning that not only is spring the sum of its parts, but it is the sum of its observers, too.

2015: Heavy snowstorms continue to cover the Northeast. Boston has no place to put the extra snow. Record amounts. Here in Yellow Springs Paula Cordell, who lives on the south end of town called: "I saw a flock of five bluebirds. I was so excited. I had to tell someone. What a great morning surprise."

2017: A major snowstorm buried the Northeast this morning as a beautiful thaw came to an end in Yellow Springs with flurries and a high only in the 20s. But Mary Sue wrote: "Just had a bunch of redwing blackbirds at our feeders, really early this year!" The photo she sent with her note shows only female red wings (along with some starlings). That should mean that the males are already here setting territories.

2018: High in the upper 40s today, the worst of the winter cold over, only a few days in the 30s in the forecast. In the fields across from Ellis Pond, close to a thousand Canada geese.

2019: St. Clare monastery near Cincinnati, sun and 20s: Robins all around. At Ellis Pond: hundreds of geese still camped in the nearby fields.

2020: At 8:00 this morning, steady cardinal and dove song, the first time I've heard them both so strong this year. At Ellis, hundreds and hundreds of geese.

2023: Listening for birds at about 7:15 this morning. Cardinals, song sparrows, maybe Carolina wrens, crows, woodpeckers, but no doves. Strong winds and record high of 65 today (68 in some parts of the area). I left the back door open this afternoon, and a mosquito got in and bit Jill.

And from Chris Walker: "As I stepped out for firewood this morning, I was stopped by the sound of a solitary spring peeper in the woods. And on a walk before lunch, another solitary frog having his Spring Song in the vernal pool—a long trill, rising to a steady note and then ending abruptly."

Journal

I moved my desk to an east window last week. It faces a hedge that once was forsythia but now has been grown over by honeysuckle and Japanese honeysuckle vines. The shrubbery encroaches on the sidewalk, which parallels High Street, and it is dense enough to block most traffic from view.

It is also dense enough to be a haven for house sparrows, and this afternoon, the snow is covering the hedge, and I sit and watch the sparrows flit from branch to branch, sometimes following one another, sometimes pecking at branches, moving back and forth in no obvious pattern, fluffing their feathers, chirping in steady rhythm that I once tracked to be the rate of my pulse. It is sparrow mating time, but I see nothing of that, only their communal, steady movement.

Yesterday, I went on a short retreat at the Monastery of St. Clare near Cincinnati, and I sat for a little more than an hour in the chapel and looked out the tall, wide windows at the trees lined with snow. I was sleepy, my mind a blank, and I dozed and stared at the woods and said mantra prayers and rested in the warmth and psychic protection of the church.

Today, I retreat to my window. The hypnotic mosaic of sparrows replaces my prayers. Absent-mindedly, my vision blurred, I witness the kaleidoscopic birds. I suspend my concerns, my focus and mindfulness, and instead of the occasional disruptive monkey mind that scatters my thoughts and feelings, a sparrow-in-the-bushes mind lulls me to peace beneath its wings.

This is the time of hidden regeneration.
Mist hangs above the ground.
Frost forms on open fields....
The season changes imperceptibly.
The early morning light is pale.
Clouds drift on the horizon.

Lam Kam Chuen

February 10th
The 41st Day of the Year

From what fact or event shall one really date the beginning of spring?

John Burroughs

Sunrise/set: 7:34/6:05
Day's Length: 10 hours 31 minutes
Average High/Low: 37/20
Average Temperature: 28
Record High: 72 – 1932
Record Low: - 22 – 1899

Weather
The 10th brings highs in the 50s or 60s on five percent of the years, and 40s in 35 percent of them. Cooler 30s, however, occur 30 percent of the time; 20s come 20 percent of the days, teens five percent, single digit highs five percent. Rain or snow falls only one year out of five. Overcast conditions remain common, however, the sun appearing only half the time. Chances of a below-zero morning: one in 20.

Natural Calendar
The flowering season has just barely begun in the warmest corners of the Ohio Valley, and one might take an early stock of the landscape before momentum builds much more.

The exact end of winter comes well before the thaws, of course, arriving unseen in the coldest weeks of the year when the March and April bulbs follow their own subterranean schedules and push up through mulch beneath the snow. Some daffodil stalks have reached two inches high, and a few tulips and hyacinths are up at least an inch. Snowdrops and aconite may be ready to bloom.

Lilac buds are swollen, fat green and gold. On the pussy willow branches, a few catkins are cracking. Garlic mustard, wild mallow and henbit are growing new leaves. Chickweed is spreading quickly. Wild strawberry, celandine, wild onions, hollyhocks, sweet William, lamb's ear, lungwort, dandelion, motherwort, and great mullein have remained intact from fall and are waiting for the retreat of the snow a little more sun.

The beauty of a seasonal inventory is that there is never a correct number of things to find. Spring is as much a state of mind as a state of nature. The end of winter always appears in the eye of the beholder. Critical mass for the arrival of spring rests less on the total quantity of observations than on one crucial scent or sight or sound that tips the scales of private time. Each person encounters that pivotal event at a different moment and in a different way. Whenever that one event occurs, then the entire scaffolding of the old year collapses, and all the pieces of the new year take on meaning as they fall into place.

Daybook

1984: Mill Habitat: a few aster leaves, some deadnettle, mint. It seems that the growth cycle is underway, if ever so slightly. Came across a group of naturalists from the college setting up to watch the nocturnal voles, "the most common mammal," they said of the Glen.

1986: Cardinal sings at 7:09 a.m.

1990: First yellow crocus bloomed downtown today. First cardinals heard at 7:15, doves at 7:20. Daffodils two to three inches in the round garden. Tulips coming up in scattered locations. New leaves on the mums. Many more garlic stalks have pushed up in the last two weeks, and they are well ahead of the new daffodils.

1993: High of 63 today. I went to the Cascades looking for signs of spring. No growth starting yet. Hepatica leaves still pale and limp, the moss short. Noticed a few green leaves from last year remaining on shrubs by the river. Driving to Clifton: seed beans still hanging from the catalpas. Hawthorns still have their red berries. Tonight a sweetness in the air, the scent of the thaw, of earth and of old leaves ready to be dug under.

1994: Three robins at the corner of Limestone and Dayton Street eating crab apples as the cars go by. Ice on the ground and a cold wind all day.

1996: After two months of deep cold, a day in the 60s, south wind, clear skies. The first moth was out. Snowdrops were up an inch, snow crocus a little more. Stonecrop had grown under the mulch, and columbine.

1998: Robins finally arrived at Wilberforce, eating hawthorn berries outside my window. Raccoon killed on Wilberforce-Clifton Road.

2000: Two sparrow hawks noticed on the way to Springfield. Have they started their spring migration?

2001: Susi's snowdrops are up, white buds waiting to open.

2004: A cardinal was singing at 7:10 this morning when I came out to start the car. After yesterday's sun and high in the upper 30s, I saw that two skunks and two raccoons had been killed last night on the roads to Washington Court House. Arriving home about 2:00 p.m., I drove right under a turkey vulture circling Corey Street.

2005: Fresh snow, continuing flurries, gray and cold. Along the way to Washington Court House, corn stubble and grasses easily rise above the minor accumulation. Ponds are still frozen, but the one pond on which the geese have stayed through the winter is still open a little.

2006: A cabbage butterfly hatched from one of the flowerpots in the greenhouse this afternoon, fluttered around at the windows. Outside, the temperature is in the 30s, intermittent sun. It wouldn't do to put him outside. On February 8, 1985, the same event: a cabbage butterfly emerged and fluttered around the windows. I pretend that as long as the temperature were favorable, cabbage butterflies everywhere would come out in the second week of February.

2008: Doves heard again this morning, this time well before dawn.

2009: Thaw continuing, the temperature beginning at 51 this morning, snow has disappeared from most of the garden space, offering a base line from which spring might be measured. After a bitter January with more than a foot of snow, the ground was frozen as much as it would ever be here in Yellow Springs, and the revival now – even if halted by more severe weather – will be applicable to the coldest years. And from such a base line, one could estimate the warmth of springs past and compare and predict progress.

Snowdrops are up an inch, and a few daffodils have emerged. Crocus leaves are tiny, their clusters even shorter than the daffodils. Poppy leaves are strong and erect. Celandine is prostrate but bright. Great mullein had been twisted by the drifts but has straightened out. Lamb's ear looks ready to put on new growth. Lenten rose leaves have been freed to sprawl and stretch. Lungwort is flat but has a few green leaves. No nubs of peonies yet, and no dove calls this morning, but when I was walking Bella through the alley, I heard the first robin whinny of the year – no longer the winter chirping and chortling. And Jeanie saw her second skunk on her morning walk with Chris.

Rick Donahoe reported a groundhog sighting: "I saw my first groundhog before noon on US 42 south of Xenia." By the end of the day, the park down the block was clear of snow, and almost all the yards along Dayton Street. The wind was still blowing from the south, and fierce winds are predicted for tomorrow as the end of the thaw moves across the Plains with tornadoes and thunderstorms.

2010: One of Jeanie's friends reports that a skunk sprayed both her dogs a few nights ago.

2011: One below zero this morning, sunny all day, not even cirrus. Mary Sue wrote me that today was the last day she saw the sandhill cranes near Ellis Pond.

2013: A cardinal was singing at 7:10 this morning when I let Monk, the cat, out. Crows at 7:30, blue jay at 8:10. Aconites are blooming behind the Danielsons' and Mrs. Timberlake's houses.

2015: Very first crow at 7:16, cardinals paired up by the feeder, making "chit" sounds. No territorial calls heard.

2018: I smelled the first skunk of the season under or near the house this morning.

2019: As I was walking back from Jill's at 9:30 or so this morning, a small murder of crows was making a racket. Then I heard a red-tailed hawk. The commotion lasted almost a quarter of an hour.

2020: Light rain and 46 degrees. The first cardinal and dove at 7:17 this morning. Leslie and Bruce reported that a "huge starling flock, at least 2,000, upward to 3,000, swarmed in the trees around our house and neighborhood, a din of squeaks and chattering."

2022: A minor thaw today, blue jays, cardinals, robins midmorning.

Journal

After a short morning walk, I am sitting in my father's old armchair, looking out the window. Waiting for seed catalogs to come in the mail. Watching cardinals and black-capped chickadees and house sparrows at the feeder. Listening for blue jay bell calls.

Remembering a poem by Jorge Guillen, a poet of the Spanish Generation of 1927, "Beato Sillón" or "Blessed/Holy Chair."

Guillen sinks into the peace of his house, his chair. "Nothing is happening," he writes. "My eyes don't see; they know. The world in well/made." The high tide of his present in that place is everything.

I hear the heater fan's white noise. I watch Moya's snow-covered roof across the way. Tangles of honeysuckle, wisteria, tree-of-heaven, rose of Sharon, bittersweet and hops divide the robin's-egg blue sky. Pussy willows have broken out way up above the street. Robins peeping. Great conversations of geese off at Ellis Pond. A Jenny wren comes to eat, quickly and carefully.

The snow I walked through this morning was crunchy and dirty Now the sidewalk is under a deep puddle. The waterfall from my blocked gutters pulses and splatters onto the front steps. Ice from the roof shatters at my door. One stink bug crawls back and forth across one pane of the north window.

Flat, dark leaves of the Lenten roses in the dooryard. Flopped goldenrod, seed tufts long gone. Fingers of euonymus vines, which choked the snowdrops this year, reach out into fallen twigs. One cluster of daffodils one-inch high. White and black, white and brown season. Restless maples, sap coming on.

For an instant, sparrows take over, fighting, crowding, attacking, pushing, flying off.
Forty-five degrees. Soft, wet wind from the southwest, sweet with spring. Barometer dropping.

Nothing is happening. I am here in my father's chair at time's high tide. The world is well/made.

February 11th
The 42nd Day of the Year

All things are engaged in writing their history… Not a footstep into the snow, or along the ground, but prints in characters more or less lasting, a map of its march. The ground is all memoranda and signatures; and every object covered over with hints. In nature, this self-registration is incessant, and the narrative is the print of the seal.

Ralph Waldo Emerson

Sunrise/set: 7:33/6:06
Day's Length: 10 hours 33 minutes
Average High/Low: 37/20
Average Temperature: 29
Record High: 69 – 1932 (64 – 2017)
Record Low: - 14 – 1885

Weather

The third cold wave of the month, ordinarily the last severe system of Late Winter, arrives near this date. And today is usually one of the wettest of the month, with snow falling 35 percent of the time, and rain another 20 percent. A sunless sky is typical: only one day in three brings any break in the clouds. Highs reach into the 50s or 60s ten percent of the time; 40s occur on 25 percent of the days, 30s on another 25 percent, 20s on 40 percent of the days. The percentages of milder weather are becoming more substantial as the month progresses, and they are decent statistical gauges for measuring the arrival of spring.

Natural Calendar

Striped bass are biting in lakes across the lower Midwest and the South. In the sun of central Florida, dragonflies are hunting. Gardeners now spray fruit trees when high temperatures climb into the 40s and freezing temperatures are expected to stay away for 24 to 48 hours.

1982: Sparrows mating along the curbs, building nests under the eaves of my roof. At the Covered Bridge, not far from the skunk cabbage, thistles are holding their own, green tops snug to the ground.

1984: Cardinals sing 7:14 a.m. Primrose begins to push new leaves up under its old frozen ones. Out Polecat Road this morning, fog hid the far shore of Ellis Pond.

1987: Late afternoon fishing, a few chubs and shiners. Ice along the edge of the river. No carp yet.

1988: First robin seen at Wilberforce.

1990: First new bulbs visible along the honeysuckle, small red tips pushing up. One rhubarb leaf, wrinkled and yellow, has emerged fully. In the greenhouse, half the mother-of-millions plants have faded. I am cutting them back.

1993: Janet Hackett reports that some of her aconites bloomed yesterday.

1994: The cold continues. Two feet of snow in New York City. The airports of the eastern seaboard have shut down. Kentucky, West Virginia, and much of the South are paralyzed by ice storms. Along the Chicago shoreline, no open water visible. Here in Yellow Springs, schools have been closed all week, the roads and walks covered with a little snow and a layer of slick ice. Temperatures have been in the teens and 20s with little letup since Christmas, and the woodpile is almost exhausted. But the evenings are longer, light well past six, and the cardinals are starting to sing all day. Mrs. Bletzinger even called this afternoon, said she had more than a dozen red-winged blackbirds at her feeder.

1998: The sedum is up in the east garden - pushed up the mulch probably a day or so ago. I found an opossum killed on the highway this morning.

1999: Cardinal at 7:15 a.m., strong. Yesterday on Stafford Street, a big red maple was opening. Mild wind all day, close to a record high in the upper 60s. Throughout town, snowdrops are in full bloom, a few purple and white crocuses, my yellow ones even getting old. Daffodils are three to five inches and hinting at budding. Grape hyacinth paces the garlic, which is pacing the daffodils. The daylilies are unraveling an inch or so, but remain hesitant. No rhubarb or bleeding heart. No real mid-season crocus.

2000: Into Springfield: crows still in their great flocks. By the cemetery pond in Yellow Springs, geese are restless, flying back and forth.

2001: Six pussy willow catkins have cracked on the front bush.

2003: Phil Hawkey called to report he saw the first turkey vulture of the year flying over town.

2006: As I walked out the back door at 7:05 this morning, a cardinal immediately started to sing.

2008: Ed Oxley, owner of downtown's Earth Rose store, called to report he had seen a turkey vulture on February 9th, five days later than he saw the first vulture in 2004. He also said that some of his snowdrops have been in full bloom for over a week and that he had a few snow crocuses open.

2009: The sixth day of the thaw: Hard rain with wind gusts, and warm last night, and the snow is gone except for a few small clumps close to the north and east sides of the house. The wind is picking up, still from the south. Ed Oxley called around 8:30 this morning, said he had flocks of snowdrops in bloom all around his property. Cardinals and blue jays calling here, no doves yet this year. This afternoon the wind speed kept increasing; it's gusting to 50 mph and more this evening with a tornado watch in effect. Last night, tornadoes killed eight in Oklahoma. Other extremes: wildfires killing hundreds in southeastern Australia.

2011: Crows heard at 7:25 this morning, sun through the day, and a slight warming, high cirrus developing as the day progressed.

2012: Light snow and a cold, gusty northwest wind. At the St. Clare Monastery northwest of Cincinnati: Birds fed heavily through the morning, a large flock of male and female cardinals, a downy woodpecker, a red-bellied woodpecker, one or more nuthatches, countless chickadees, many juncos, house finches, goldfinches. And I am curious about the cardinal flocking, that may be the reason they have not been singing here is because they are still together, and that may have something to do with the warm winter.

2013: Sun and hard southwest wind, barometer low, temperature in the low 50s. Very strong odor of skunk in the backyard before dawn. Aconites continuing to open in the alley, one snowdrop in the east garden just barely opening. Crows at 7:22 this morning, but I missed the cardinals. Titmice heard off and on today, and for several days recently. At Ellis Pond, the white ducks have been gone ever since the water first froze over in December. Today, a green-headed duck was swimming there. In the greenhouse, Jeanie's jasmine has just started to bloom, the first white flower so fragrant.

2014: Midmorning blue jays, titmice, cardinals, sparrows. No doves heard since the beginning of the cold spell after the Groundhog Day thaw.

2015: Crows at 7:16, then silence from them as the sharp calls of a hawk seemed to put an end to other bird activity. First dove at the feeder this winter.

2016: Deep cold settles across the Midwest and the East, the cruelest weather of the winter so far.

2017: Warm in the middle 60s today, more hellebores in bloom (several white hellebore blossoms spreading their petals wide), more snowdrops fully open. The first snow crocus, five violet ones, opened under Janet's redbud tree. (I had transplanted them by accident with the hydrangea last fall – and then here they were the first of the year!) I found one peony spear up a full inch. One chickweed flower seen, and the ground was greening with more chickweed and the basal foliage of bittercress and creeping Charley. Returning from Cincinnati (where it was at least 70), a saw a Late Winter murmuration of starlings swooping across and around the freeway. In John Bryan State Park, someone had set up pails to collect maple sap.

2019: Light mist, fog, temperature at 35 degrees, melting snow. Cardinals full song when I went out to walk Ranger at 7:12 this morning. Song sparrows near Stafford Street at 7:20, a blue jay in the alley at 7:25, crows at 7:35.

2020: Soft, light snow, mild, doves heard when I went outside to walk Ranger at 7:14, cardinals 7:17. The first phase of the morning chorus is definitely underway. Some daffodils up at least six inches, a few snowdrops leaning with their white buds poised to open. On the way to Cincinnati: a hefty murmuration of starlings. Leslie reports thousands of grackles settled in her trees for a while today, and Liz wrote that starlings had arrived at her feeder.

2023: First dove heard around noon today.

Journal

The space between the unpredictable phases of Late Winter sometimes allows me a certain disconnection, a feeling similar to what I experience when I am completely free of obligations, or when everything is suddenly beyond my control.

The fact that the advance of external spring is outside of my power gives me an excuse to imagine that I do not have influence in matters of internal spring. Allowing myself to be caught at the crossroads of inter-seasonal ambivalence, I willingly give up my autonomy for a neutral sanctuary.

My anticipation about the approach of equinox and regret at the end of my winter hibernation clash like the frontal dichotomies of Late Winter weather, and a resultant stalemate spins me into a temporal and spatial slough, an eye of the storm.

Or it is as if the end of the road were still a ways off, as though I were safely between home and my destination, as though there were still plenty of time, as though the moment of truth had been delayed indefinitely.

My clear January orientation has been shunted away by the split personality of the current landscape, its signals and signs mixed, pointing one way and then another. Caught between the first warm snowdrops and the daffodil snows, I lose control over which way I am going, and I take on the ambivalence of nature, pretending to imitate it, riding that excuse at this peak of freedom in which the past hides and the future is unimagined, in which I, for a moment, live suspended above concern and judgment.

February 12th
The 43rd Day of the Year

Yet still on every side we trace the hand
Of Winter in the land,
Save where the maple reddens on the lawn,
Flushed by the season's dawn.

Henry Timrod

Sunrise/set: 7:32/6:07
Day's Length: 10 hours 35 minutes
Average High/Low: 37/20
Average Temperature: 29
Record High: 64 – 1884
Record Low: - 12 – 1889

Weather

Today's distribution of high temperatures: five percent chance of 60s (and from now on, there is at least a five percent chance of a day in the 60s on all but six of the remaining days in February, making today one more pivot date in the progress toward Early Spring), 20 percent chance of 40s, thirty-five percent of 30s, twenty percent of 20s, twenty percent of teens. Snow falls on better than 40 percent of all the days, and skies are completely overcast half the time. Below-zero lows rarely occur in Yellow Springs this morning.

Natural Calendar

Everything that is in the heavens, on the earth, and under the earth, is penetrated with connectedness, is penetrated with relatedness.

Hildegard of Bingen

Cardinals began their mating calls before dawn in the last week of Deep Winter. Now, if the weather is mild, they are in full song by seven in the morning, sometimes sing all day. Sparrows compete for mates and nesting sites, chattering and chirping in the honeysuckles. Moss grows thicker, sometimes flowers on logs in the sun.

1984: Jog to Ellis Pond. Two formations of geese fly over. Deer at the water. Ducks restless in the warm morning air. Crocus leaves have emerged at home, no flowers yet.

1986: Cardinals singing 7:05 a.m. when I went out to walk Roo, the dog.

1988: Three robins, a pair of tufted titmice, and a handful of starlings huddled in the tree outside my window at work.

1990: Crocus sprouts pushing up all over the yard.

1993: Mrs. Bletzinger reports seeing a red-winged blackbird at her platform feeder on the 10th. More aconites seen, a whole patch of them in bloom in front of Dr. Poortinga's on Xenia Avenue. About a fourth of the pussy willows on our bush are open.

1994: To Jacoby: the swamp still frozen over in some places, I was to free to walk where I wanted, right up to the clusters of fat and firm skunk cabbage, red and orange speckled, in the open rivulets, nestled in the cress. Cardinals were singing up the ridge and along the river. I heard a blue jay, and several calls of a flicker or a pileated woodpecker. Here in the swamp (where I've told Jeanie I'd like my ashes scattered after I die), in spite of the cold wind and the gray sky and ice, I felt untouched by winter. There was something healing about the way the land lay open all around me. The shallow streams were running, even when the temperature was below zero. The cress, which surpassed even the ragwort, garlic mustard, and ragwort foliage in winter hardiness and visibility, remained green and supple. They all defied the bitterness around them, and stolidly stood up to February. Coming home, I saw a herd of maybe a dozen deer at the far edge of a cornfield.

1998: First mother-of-millions plant is done flowering for the year.

1999: Last night a thunderstorm. Today, snow and wind. The fire glows in the stove in front of me.

2000: Crows at 7:25 a.m., no cardinals in the mornings, no doves. Most of the snow has melted off in the past two days, and the pond has thawed, but the days are quiet and cold. Along the west wall, daffodils are pushing an inch through the snow, maybe came up in December, like the daffodils in the east garden, before the cold weather hit.

2004: Doves heard for the first time this year; they were calling when I went outside a little before 7:00 a.m. On the way home from school, I drove past a buzzard feeding on roadkill along Grinnell Road.

2005: The first two purple snow crocuses bloomed in the sunny east garden this morning, were waiting for us after we got back from the Second Street Market. Along the south wall, one golden crocus was open. The snowdrops are still budding, getting taller, inching slowly up.

2008: A snow and ice storm continues moving up northeast from Kentucky, and the schools are closed. No birdsong today, although the sparrows and starlings are thick at the feeder. Yesterday morning, the barometer was at 30.42 and still rising a little, temperature in the single digits. Now, 24 hours later, it is at 29.90. The sky was hazy at sunrise yesterday, and the haze thickened throughout the morning until the sun was barely visible. The barometer fell to 29.30 by evening, and the stratus clouds were thick overhead. Snow began after midnight, but only a couple of inches and some freezing rain have fallen by noon.

2009: The wind blew all night, shifting to the west, and now the sky is clear, the air quite cold, the thaw almost over, winter returning. The storm has moved into the Northeast. A cardinal sang when I walked outside at 7:30, and I heard another robin whinny when I walked Bella a little later. This evening, Orion full in the south, mild, steady west wind.

2010: I heard a cardinal at 7:15 this morning, just a few minutes after the crows. In spite of a foot of snow on the ground, a skunk was out tonight, odor drifting along High Street when I walked

Bella after dark.

2012: Partly cloudy and low in the teens. Crows at 7:17 this morning. No early morning cardinal song.

2013: Mild, mostly cloudy, a little below freezing. When I went outside at 7:02 this morning with Bella, the cardinal in the yard was just warming up. At 7:07, crows called. Throughout my walk in the twilight, cardinals and crows kept me company. Early this afternoon (with a sunny high of 50), the first small violet snow crocus opened in the east garden, surrounded by the slender foliage of so many others. Then when I got home from the studio about 4:00, I heard a dove calling. And when I went out to the back yard for some wood, a grackle – the first I've seen in the yard for months – hopped up on the fence, and then a robin flew up from the honeysuckles into the box elder tree. Did the grackle and the robin come together?

Thoughts today about the romanticism of solitary nature observations, the isolation of Thoreauvian journaling about what is happening in the land, the sense of private revelation and discovery. The act of journaling itself is, of course, a sharing as well as an inner walking. But sometimes the collection and the compilation of the experience of others can expand and extend the personal encounter with seasonal change. Whether through readings or reports from other observers, the secret, hidden romance can be deepened, enhanced and mellowed. And maybe I have carried that social context more than I've realized, and maybe it has shaped this daybook from the very beginning. So my interest in collecting quotations and observations from other people has simply been a way of finding out how I should be alone with nature, informed and accompanied by the minds of other travelers.

2014: The weather gradually moderating after most of the month remaining below freezing. I saw the robin drinking from the pond again today, the pond heater keeping the fish and the bird alive.

2019: From Flying Mouse Farms, Michele Burns reports that the sap started to flow today. Hard wind gusts tonight, trees creaking, leaves crackling as they flew about when I walked Ranger around

9:00.

2020: Jenny sent videos of grackles all over her trees just outside of town.

2021: Stability of deep cold continues, one robin visiting the pond waterfall on many mornings, no sap running at the Flying Mouse, wood pile dwindling, six to ten inches of snow on the ground for over a week, more snow forecast, maybe up to a foot, for next week. The birds eat heartily, one white-throated sparrow noticed in the mass of house sparrows, numerous cowbirds. One tufted titmouse (the first I've seen this winter) visited yesterday. Reading through the entry of this day from 2013, I think about Ed Oxley and how sad I am to lose him, one of the many personae (friends) of this record.

2023: Another dove heard today, steady calling, their conversations underway. A pair of geese on screeching upriver at the Covered Bridge. Few signs in the undergrowth there, only chickweed and once in a while small ragwort leaves, bright and soft.

Here is the glory of created things,
The earth and the sky,
The sun and the moon,
The stars and the vast expanses:
Here is fellowship with all that was created,
The air and the wind,
Cloud and rain,
Sunshine and snow.

Euros Bowen, from "Gloria"

February 13th
The 44th Day of the Year

Yet spring was in the mild air warmed by meager sunshine, and swelling buds of soft maple along the creek glowed a dull red. The scent in the air was not of flowers but of sun-warmed slopes and muddy shores, promising fertility and summer growth.

Harlan Hubbard

Sunrise/set: 7:31/6:08
Day's Length: 10 hours 37 minutes
Average High/Low: 37/21
Average Temperature: 29
Record High: 70 – 1938
Record Low: - 28 – 1899

Weather

February 13th brings a higher chance (a 50 percent chance) for highs only in the 30s than any other day of the month. On the other hand, 60s occur five percent of the time, 50s five percent, 40s fifteen percent, 20s twenty percent and teens five percent. There is a 35 percent for rain or snow, and a 50/50 chance of totally overcast skies. Below-zero lows occur just once in a decade

Natural Calendar

The shift in weather that multiplies the signs of spring takes place in the middle of February nine out of ten of the years in my record. Three or four good thaws, sometimes lasting a week apiece, have already come up from the South before then.

Sunrise has moved up half an hour since solstice, bird song from 7:30 a.m. to 7:00 a.m. Dusk, on a clear day, can go past 7:00 p.m. Cardinals not only sing before dawn, but deep into the afternoon. Peonies grow taller through the mulch, their deep red tips emerging when blue jays are calling, and sparrows and starlings are loud and reckless in the middle of mating.

1983: Basal leaves of thistles at South Glen have held their own through the winter.

1986: Winter breaking apart, tulips, crocus coming up. Foliage of ragwort, hemlock, dock seems to be stronger.

1987: Cardinals sing all morning and into the afternoon. Daffodils and tulips up two inches downtown. Mother-of-millions still blooming in the greenhouse. There has been an increase in geranium blooms over the past week or so. Large river chub, about a foot long, caught late this afternoon at Sycamore Hole.

1990: High of 65 today. Pussy willows almost half open, just like in 1984. Pyrethrums are growing new variegated leaves, poppies much stronger.

1991: Ash Wednesday. Two opossums and a raccoon killed along the highway. First fly gets into my classroom. Thousands of crows in Springfield for the past weeks. One worm crossed the sidewalk in the rain this morning, the first of the year.

1993: An inch of snow covers all the aconites. Daffodils have pushed up two inches this past week. Time to cover them with straw. Sparrows loud all afternoon.

1994: At the mill dam, into Mint Hollow: I heard the call again of what I thought would be a flicker or pileated woodpecker, then I saw it a few hundred yards away, a pileated, huge, long and thin.

1998: First bluebird seen today. She zoomed in front of the car as I just turned down Grinnell Road. The cats killed a small camel cricket last night in the greenhouse.

2000: When I went out to get wood at 6:00 this morning, I heard the screech owl back over near Limestone Street. At 7:10, I went to the back door, heard a cardinal sing in the dark. Got dressed and went walking; by 7:15 cardinals and crows loud all around the village. Titmouse heard at 7:23. When I went out again to let the dog out at 8:35, starlings were in full song; but I missed the time they started. Skunk killed on Dayton-Yellow Springs Road last night.

2001: One opossum seen on the way to Springfield.

2004: Cardinals were singing when I went outside at 7:15 this morning.

2005: Roadkills are increasing throughout the countryside with temperatures in the 40s and 50s during the afternoons. A skunk, a groundhog and several opossums seen this weekend on the highways. Jeanie even saw an opossum running around outside the bedroom window late this morning.

Taking inventory in the yard, I found that many daffodils had reached two inches high, and a few tulips were up at least an inch. The lilac buds were swollen, fat green and gold. On the old pussy willow branches, a few catkins were cracking. Garlic mustard clusters were growing new leaves. The monarda patch showed half-inch foliage. Chickweed was greening in the garden. Wild strawberry foliage and celandine were intact under the snow. No red rhubarb or peony stalks are up yet. Forsythia and honeysuckles, the earliest shrubs, still keep their buds tightly wrapped. The longer the list of plants observed in February inventory, the greater the context for the subtle alterations of each day ahead, the more exciting each addition.

2007: A strong storm system has paralyzed the country from Nebraska all the way to New York. Tornadoes have appeared in the South. It has snowed here since before dawn, six inches on the ground, and now sleet. The entire region has shut down. Even the Air Force base is closed.

2008: The storm that closed most of Yellow Springs yesterday has moved into the Northeast. Here, the air is cold and landscape is quiet, no cardinals or doves singing this morning, only a few crows about 7:40. The cold weather has definitely inhibited the rhythm of territorial calls this winter. On the other hand, Tat e-mailed from Wisconsin to tell me that her friend near Janesville heard her first cardinal of the year today and that chickadees are "doing their mating chirping."

2009: Finally a calm morning, almost no wind at all. The sky is clear, the waning moon in the east. Faint calls of cardinals and doves near 7:00 this morning , then a strong, obvious dove song at 8:15, along with many blue jay bell calls, robin clucks, cardinal calls and chirps from starlings in Don's tree. In the east dooryard garden, many clumps of snowdrops are up now, all with white tips. Along the north garden, celandine and tall ragwort have put on quite a bit of growth, the power of last week's thaw seeming to have a kind of residual strength that pulls leaves out in spite of the cool weather now.

2010: Two skunks killed on Dayton Street last night – even with the low in the teens and deep snow. One buzzard circling the neighborhood this afternoon.

2012: A cardinal heard at 7:15 this morning when I let the cat out into the back yard - the first pre-dawn cardinal song this year. And when I walked Bella at 9:30, a tufted titmouse sang all the way down Dayton Street, and a cardinal and a dove sang to me on Stafford Street. Coming home, I saw two sparrows mating on the front sidewalk. More cardinals at 1:30 this afternoon and then an hour later, too. Snow forecast for tonight.

2013: At John Bryan Park before 7:00 a.m.. No birds until I got home at 7:15 – then cardinals and crows all around. I heard a dove calling about 9:00. Along Stafford Street, aconites are in early bloom At Ellis Pond, about a hundred and fifty Canadian geese floated quietly on the water, having left their usual habitat of the field across the road. A lone buzzard over Yellow Springs this afternoon.

2015: Cloudy, 20s, first cardinal at 7:17 a.m. No crows , though.

2017: Sun and chilly today, and algae growing in the pond, turning the water a translucent green, even with the water in the 40s. People are tapping maple trees all around the college campus.

Crows raucous in the early afternoon, Squill foliage up an inch or two, and a few lips of tulips. Pruning of honeysuckles, tree of heaven and the crab apple tree completed.

2018: A vast changeup in weather for the eastern half of the country, Early Spring spreading across the land from the Mississippi north and south and east. Blue jays and titmice calling off and on.

2019: High only near freezing this afternoon, hard wind at Ellis Pond, geese hunkered down in the sun.

2021: I went outside at 7:03 with Ranger. As we made our way through the alley snow (at least six inches deep), the first cardinals sang out at 7:07 and continued throughout our walk. Crows woke up at 7:10, and a red-shouldered hawk cried out above us at 7:11.

2023: Robin whinny heard in the yard this morning, adding to the accumulation of spring in these warm days. Mary Sue reports: "We had red-winged blackbirds arrive this morning, earlier than the last several years. We also had a very unusual early visit back in December during that deep freeze." Jill told me she thought she heard the red-wings yesterday at the wetlands, but she wasn't able to see them. Then I saw Tracy Logan at the flower shop: He had seen red-winged blackbirds five days ago! And then Emily wrote: She had seen sandhill cranes flying over the Glen today, must be heading north?

Journal
Lord and gentle Maker,
Move the Axis of the Season
From the troubled Winter.
Wake the fertile Beauty
Of the tawny Flowers,
And restore your Pleasure
To the Pastures of the Spring.

Vespers Hymn, Tuesday before Ash Wednesday

Earth turns toward spring past February's Cross-Quarter Day. Every year the circular story is about death to life, beginning quietly in the tomb of snow. Every year, the plot is the same, always certain, always beautiful, always about the same length, requiring only a little experience or a little trust to see it through to the climax of April.

My personal reading hangs on details that I find, imagine and collect. The more I see and fit into place, the more intricate and intriguing the story's episodes. Knowing the outcome never spoils the watching. Each time I read it, the chronicle is enhanced by my anticipation and by new patterns of change in the weather as well as in myself.

The waiting of the prelude also reminds me of my own waiting. The transformation of winter to spring is not separate from me. While I believe in the resurgent flowering of the landscape, I am not so sure about what will happen to me or what I will choose to do or be. The story often reassures me, but never quite enough. I have to let go blindly into a willing suspension of doubt or disbelieve and ride the season the way it comes, identifying with all its floral characters, and so feel relief and satisfaction and happiness at the pleasure of the close, which opens still another story and another self to be.

February 14th
The 45th Day of the Year

In Nature nothing is insignificant, nothing ignoble, nothing sinful, nothing repetitious. All the music is great music, all the lines have meaning.

Donald Culross Peattie

Sunrise/set: 7:30/6:10
Day's Length: 10 hours 40 minutes
Average High/Low: 38/21
Average Temperature: 29
Record High: 67 – 1918
Record Low: - 9 – 1905

Weather
Today is the first day of Early Spring throughout the Lower Midwest. Although temperatures can be in the 30s forty-five percent of the time or even in the 20s on five percent of all the days, February 14th suddenly offers a 50 percent chance of highs above 40 degrees: in the 40s forty-five percent of the time, in the 50s or 60s the remaining five percent. Precipitation is often the price for moderation: snow falls 25 percent of the years, rain another 30 percent. And from this point forward in the year, rain is more likely to fall than snow. Odds for a morning below zero are less than five percent per day for the 14th through the 16th.

Natural Calendar
Depending on the year, growth occurs on ragwort, dock, sweet rocket, asters, winter cress, poison hemlock, sedum, mint, celandine, plantain, poppies, pansies, daffodils, tulips, crocus, aconite, hyacinth and strawberries. All those hardy leaves are expanding a centimeter here or there, such measurements seeming unimportant until they can measure spring, and then there is no insignificant degree. The signs accelerate, accumulate, and become a new season, turning into what they represent by force of numbers. Then, what at first looks the same as any winter day is really a day in Early Spring. The wind is still raw, and the grass

and the trees are brown, but the balance has tipped. The thaws are preserved, their effects impervious to the steady progression of cold fronts, and suddenly winter collapses into giving birth.

Daybook

1983: Tulips and daffodils coming up along the front fence. Crocus leaves a couple of inches.

1988: Walk at South Glen. Cardinals singing. Woodpeckers loud. Bluebirds seen past Sycamore hole. Small black-green insect out crawling on top of the snow. Craneflies spinning in the sun. Fishing holes frozen over.

1993: Blue jays loud this morning, seem to be getting louder all the time. Crows calling from dawn into mid morning. Sparrows fighting. Snow on the ground, flurries through the day, but all the sounds belong to spring.

1994: Finally blue sky, pure turquoise, and sun to warm us into the 40s for the first time in weeks. The ice on the campus melted in a few hours this afternoon. I could walk on the bare ground, felt firm as if I'd gotten off a boat onto dry land. A sense of relief all day. Coming home: a ruckus of sparrows, more noise than I've heard from them all winter.

1998: Descending whinny of a screech owl south past Limestone Street this morning at about 6:30, moon setting over the locust trees. The daffodils are three inches now, two golden crocus in full bloom in the south garden, purple deadnettle blooms by the pond, garlic five inches, pussy willows opening maybe a fourth to a third of the way.

1999: Crow at 7:05 a.m. Skies clear. Very cold.

2001: Walking Buttercup in the cold rain after dark, went past the Webb's old house: a good clump of snowdrops in full bloom.

2005: A dove was calling at 7:10 this morning, the morning mild and cloudy, wind high. The first robin heard in the back yard at

9:35.

2008: The sense of potential now, the gathering spring, the great winds of change, the storms of March and April, the conflagrations to come, all of the power of the sun about to be unleashed.

2009: Winterberries are falling heavily now; bittersweet berries are down to just a fraction of their autumn numbers; coralberries have lost their color, are all dull brown. On my walk this morning, robins, cardinals and blue jays were singing. On the road to Cincinnati, I saw one buzzard circling Byron, and a number of roadkills: three skunks, three raccoons, two opossums, all quite small. In the woods by the monastery, a pileated woodpecker was calling throughout my walk in the late morning.

2011: Crows at 7:11 this morning, strong smell of skunk when I went out to the shed. Neysa and Ivano saw eight deer in the village park this afternoon, and they saw a skunk roadkill on the way to Springfield.

2012: Crows at 7:16 this morning, light snow falling, temperature in the 20s. No cardinals heard at dawn, but one or two singing near the alley at 9:00. The afternoon warming up, the pond ice turning gray and pocked, slushy at the west end.

2013: As I waited outside in the twilight this morning, a distant cardinal sang at 7:05. Crows were late, 7:35. For the second morning in a row, a dove was calling around 9:00. At Jacoby with Jeff in the midmorning: five robins seen on the hillside above the canoe launch, skunk cabbage blooming in places in the bottomland. I checked the hellebores after lunch: one of them has an open white flower, many buds. A buzzard seen swooping across the sky south of Ellis Pond late in the afternoon, riding the steady southwest wind, and at least a hundred geese were floating in the quiet water.

2014: This morning, mild and mostly clear, I walked out the door at exactly 7:00, and I was met with a burst of cardinal song not a dozen feet from where I stood. Then crows followed immediately afterward, and all the birds accompanied my walk. This afternoon and evening, more and more snow.

2017: First grackle seen at the feeder this morning around 9:00 (the second-earliest I've seen them – the first on February 12, 2013). First yellow crocus open at Jill's house. A second clump of violet crocus blooming at home, this one at the south wall. The first lungwort leaves came up over night. Under the old peach tree, the first two buds in a daffodil cluster, a planting several years old. Many peony tips now showing, many hyacinth, daffodil, day lily and squill leaves pushing out of the ground. A handful of turkey vultures circling the village.

2019: Temperature in the upper 30s, light overcast sky. First cardinal heard at 7:08 this morning. Blue jays sparring at the back feeders.

2023: Jill reports that stinkbugs are back at her house. When we walked at Clifton Gorge late in the afternoon, we heard geese calling and one pair was guarding a place along the river. In the dooryard and in sunny spots along Limestone Street, snowdrops are fuly developed, bells open and facing the ground, Audrey reports aconites blooming since January, and now red-winged blackbirds. Emily saw redwings today, too.

It's an earth song –
And I've been waiting long
For an earth song.
It's a spring song!
I've been waiting long
For a spring song:
Strong as the busting of young buds.
Strong as the shoots of a new plant
Strong as the coming of the first child
From its mother's womb –
An earth song!
A body song!

A spring song!
And I've been waiting long
For an earth song.

Langston Hughes

February 15th
The 46th Day of the Year

Spring arrives when it arrives; when the snowdrops show buds; chickweed puts forth its tiny blooms; the pussy willows show brilliant white tips against the brown-black buds; the bluebird's haunting, illusive quavering call is borne on a February wind; skunk cabbage shows a deep blackish-purple tip through soggy ice....

Charles Burchfield, *Journal*

Sunrise/set: 7:28/6:11
Day's Length: 10 hours 43 minutes
Average High/Low: 38/21
Average Temperature: 29
Record High: 69 – 1954, 71 – 2023
Record Low: - 3 – 1905

Weather
Today has the highest incidence of highs in the 50s and 60s (and even of 70) of any time so far in February - a full 40 percent of the afternoons reach those levels (with a 15 percent chance of 60s, and 25 percent of 50s). That's the first time since December 15th that the likelihood of mild temperatures has been so great. And those statistics provide a neat numerical parenthesis to winter: December 15th is the pivot date for the arrival of really severe weather in the region; February 15th is obviously the spring pivot date. Of course, cooler highs do occur: the chances of 40s: fifteen percent; 30s come 25 percent of the time, 20s fifteen percent and teens five percent. Snow falls 20 percent of the days, rain another fifteen percent; skies are completely overcast half the time

The Week Ahead
The third quarter in February is statistically one of the most exciting of the entire year. Chances of highs in the 20s or below remain low at 20 percent during the first part of the week, and then, for the first time since late November, fall to almost

nothing by the end of the week. Chances of highs in the 40s or above climb to 80 percent by the 20th, and then between the 18th and the 23rd, chances of highs in the 50s or 60s reaches an average of 35 percent per day, the first time that has happened since December 10th. And in one of the most radical weather changes of the year, the weekly chances of an afternoon in the 60s swell from last week's one in ten to five in ten.

Although below-zero temperatures can occur at this time of the year, February's third quarter is the second-last period of Early Spring in which such cold might be expected (March's first week is the very last). Even the fifth high- pressure system of the month, which passes through around the 20th, is typically a mild one. There is a 30 percent chance of precipitation on most days this week. The 20th is the day least likely to be wet, bringing just a 20 percent chance of rain or snow. The likelihood for clouds is high: 60 percent of the days offer no sun at all. The average amount of snowfall for this week is ordinarily the lowest of the month.

The Natural Calendar

Even though the February 15th high-pressure ridge can be disappointing to those most in need of spring, the aftermath of this cold wave brings increasing odds for the best thaw so far in the year. Across the South, the floral cycle has started near this time, and along the Canadian border, the frequency of highs in the teens or below starts to drop. The season of spring birdsong begins most years by January 25, but it is the middle of February that consistently turns Late Winter into Early Spring. Sometimes the weather doesn't change for the better in the early days of the year's second month; sometimes the cold is worse than in the middle of January. But the sound changes and fills the silence of dormancy, songs accumulating like spring leaves.

Daybook

1984: More than half of the pussy willows have opened.

1985: Robin heard this afternoon.

1988: Cardinals were in full song from around 7:00 a.m. until sundown today.

1991: Four inches of snow on the ground, the earth bright even with the moon new. I'd forgotten about the lightness of the night in a snowy winter, and the darkness of the ground in spring.

1992: Long flocks of starlings seen as I drove through Illinois and western Indiana. Trees are flowering in Jacksonville, Florida, says Jeni, and the pollen is heavy on the trees around her building.

1993: The biggest snow of the year is due tomorrow. Birds have been feeding heavily all day, especially the starlings, swarming around the suet like bees.

1999: Cardinal sang at 7:03 this morning, sky almost dark. Crows heard at 7:08. Around the yard, the south garden's snow crocus has all wilted now, replaced by the standard golds and purples. At the Cascades by a fallen log, the first hepatica flower was three-fourths open, some small new hepatica leaves out too.

2000: As I came out of the house this morning to get wood at about 9:00, I heard cardinals all around the yard. Then at 9:25 as I was working at my desk, the first bell call of the blue jay came indoors strong and sharp.

2002: Daylilies are one to two inches tall. Daffodils are six inches, and many are budded. Snow crocus, aconites, and snowdrops are in full bloom. Forsythia buds are swelling, showing a little bright yellow.

2005: Sun and highs in the middle 60s today. Three purple crocus are blooming in the east garden. A few snowdrop buds have come undone, and the very first two red peony stalks are visible. On the way to Washington Court House this morning, the air was mild, and the sky was a pale yellow and peach. Water in the ditches was shining. Above: benign cirrus. Across the fields: smoky gray. The ice on the ponds had melted over the past few days, only a black patina of frozen water remaining.

2006: With a high of 60 today, several snowdrop buds emerged from their sheaths. One yellow snow crocus bloomed in the east garden, two in the south garden.

2007: Cold but mostly sunny today. I heard a cardinal at 7:10 this morning, crows about 15 minutes later. Titmice calling throughout my walk in the alley.

2009: Sunny and 25 degrees, no wind. Doves were singing at 7:00, crows and a distant cardinal calling, and when I walked Bella in the alley at 8:15, I was surrounded by loud robinsong, cardinalsong, and dovesong. If the weather is cold for the next few days, the landscape may not change, but it will be easy to listen and know that it is Early Spring. Talked to Tat this morning in Wisconsin: she still has a foot of snow on the ground, but her cardinals are singing. She has no robins or doves yet. A skunk crossed High Street in front of me as I drove over to the Browns' house around 7:15 this evening.

2010: The third major snowstorm this month has brought another eight inches of snow!

2011: The thaw continues, snow half melted over the past few days. Crows were awake at 6:56 this morning, the earliest I've heard them this year. Faint odor of skunk before dawn. Spears of snowdrops and a few daffodils finally visible. A groundhog was hit within a day or so along Dayton-Yellow Springs Road.

2012: Crows at 7:20 this morning, cardinals by 7:45 and then on through the morning. I found a woolly bear caterpillar exploring the front porch, even with the temperature at freezing. Under the redbud tree, two primroses have buds tucked tightly among the high leaves. In the south garden, all the violet snow crocus are budded, waiting for sun.

2015: Liz writes to report the sighting of a yellow-bellied sapsucker on her maple tree: "It was a juvenile female, based on the coloring and markings. About this time last year I also saw one, same place."

2016: Fog settles in over the land, soft breath of the arrival of Early Spring. Starlings still cluster along the telephone lines. Dimmy reported seeing juncos at her feeder for the first time this winter a week or so ago. They haven't been in my yard at all.

2018: South from Yellow Springs to Athens, Alabama: Departure in mild 50-degree weather, almost all the snow melted after the thaw and rain of the last two days. In the circle garden, daffodils were up a couple of inches, snowdrops with white tips, one with a large bud. The landscape brown all the way through Louisville, Kentucky but at a rest stop, daffodils were up at least six inches. Then near Bowling Green, winter grain fields started to turn green, and the greening of the fields and roadsides grew and grew as the weather warmed into the upper 70s through Tennessee. In the woods behind our hotel in Athens, Alabama, just over the Tennessee border, tree frogs were steady and loud. Pansies were blooming in front of a restaurant.

2019: The temperatures have been up and down, but daffodils are four inches around the yard, and the circle garden is coming alive with hyacinth sprouts. At Ellis Pond, all the geese (about 250) have left the field across the road and have gathered at the pond, feeding along the shore, avoiding me and Ranger when we approach, John Rudolf reported seeing sandhill cranes heading southwest today.

2020: I heard the first blue jay bell call this morning around 7:45. Walking home from the Glass Farm wetland (no red-winged blackbirds yet), Jill and I saw a vast flock of birds along the southern horizon, the flock stretching all the way across the sky, east to west, passing for several minutes.

2021: The chilly February continues, almost a foot of snow on the ground and temperatures remaining well below freezing, placing this week in the 15 percent for cold. A robin comes before dawn to drink from the pond waterfall that is still running. Before lunch, I stood at the back door watching the birds at the feeders and talking to Jill on the pone when suddenly a hawk swooped across from my left and swept up a dove from the ground. A puff of feathers and they were gone. A few minutes later, the first bird to return was a tufted titmouse. Then chickadees. Then the sparrows came back, then a male cardinal. All as if nothing had happened

Snow is on the way, and I went back to my barometric graphs and daybook notes from February 1993. That month started out so warm, then ended with more than a week of below freezing temperatures and heavy snows. Tomorrow is the anniversary of the nine-inch blizzard from that year. And today in 2010 brought a snowstorm, too.

2023: Green flush on honeysuckle and quince buds. For the first time in decades, my pussy willow trees have died: no pussy willows here this year.

2023: Gray, rainy and mild in the 50s today. The snowdrops and hellebores in the dooryard are in full flower now, as are the aconites throughout the village. This February 16 is the height of those seasons. Tat reports snow in Madison, Wisconsin. A cold snap is due tonight.

True magic, she told him, was the sacramental act of turning a sign into what it signified. She added that such grace was not only the common stuff of literature and liturgy but the way of Nature herself.

Darla Peyton

February 16th
The 47th Day of the Year

Now nourish soil with fattening dung,
Now scatter grimy ashes on the wasted plot.

Virgil

Sunrise/set: 7:27/6:12
Day's Length: 10 hours 45 minutes
Average High/Low: 38/21
Average Temperature: 30
Record High: 72 – 1883
Record Low: - 3 – 1885

Weather

Today's high temperatures are in the 50s twenty percent of the time, and in the 40s another 25 percent. Thirties come 35 percent of the years, 20s fifteen percent, teens five percent. The sky is overcast more than 60 percent of the time, with snow falling one day out of five, rain coming once a decade. Mornings below zero are rare.

Natural Calendar

The first week of Early Spring is often mild, bringing the first flowers into bloom, but the snow and cold waves of the year's first months may have delayed or covered many of the obvious signs of change. For guidance about the progress of the season, the groundhog is a fickle prophet, rarely emerging to prognosticate so early. Other creatures, however, take up the slack, most notably the skunk.

Skunks wander lawns and streets throughout the year, but their body clocks bring them out most frequently during their mating time of Late Winter and Early Spring. Even the most casual observer cannot miss their announcement that winter is almost over. By about the tenth week of the year, the mating cycle of the skunk comes to a close, its odor ceding to visual and auditory markers of the new season: the robin chorus before dawn, emerging pussy willows, rising daffodil spears, blooming snowdrops and aconites.

By this time in February, Procyon, the largest star of Canis Minor, replaces the Dog Star due south near 10:00 p.m. Above it, the twins of Gemini, Castor and Pollux tell of Early Spring. To their right, Orion and the Milky Way have shifted deep into the west, and the Big Dipper has moved well into the northeastern sky - up from its low December and January position - and its pointers, the outside stars of the dipper, are easily found. And by midnight, the first stars of middle summer's Hercules appear in the northeast.

Daybook

1983: Birds singing by 7:00 a.m. At South Glen, a few multiflora leaf buds have opened. More opossums and a rabbit run down on Grinnell Road. Fishermen out at the Covered Bridge.

1984: Another tan moth seen this afternoon. Poison hemlock is bushy and lush.

1989: Signs are accumulating, spring a matter of quantity, numbers of sprouts, numbers of leaves, birds, landmark after landmark. When one of the signs is present, the others are there too. Each sign becomes a gauge for the rest of the cycle, standing for the gathering of signs.

1990: Some pussy willows in front of the house have emerged completely. Maple buds are swelling. After heavy rains, the Little Miami River is flooding into the pasture at the Covered Bridge. Cardinals have been singing late into the afternoon outside my window at Wilberforce. Tulips are up three inches, daffodils, four, garlic four to six inches, so many things pushing out.

1993: The snow came without barometric warning; today has been the most wintry day of the year. Will the aconites live through the cold of the next few days?

1994: Into South Glen, late afternoon, the river high and muddy, temperatures warming into the low 40s. In the woods, there was still snow on the paths and on the northerly sides of some of the bigger hills. But coming out onto the flat, open butterfly preserve, I felt like I was literally coming to the edge of winter. The snow trail quickly tapered to icemelt, and as I walked southeast into the sun, the brown grass caught the light so that the ground turned gold ahead of me, shining promise of spring.

1999: Crows at 6:59 a.m., clear skies, cardinals at least by 7:05, probably earlier. First dove heard. Tulip, daffodil, poppy foliage coming on strong.

2000: The ice on the river had broken up, and the great thaw was underway. My bulldog, Buttercup, and I followed the paths up and along the hills. It was late in the afternoon. The sky had been gray all day, now was darker with storm clouds. We walked through flurries, sometimes a shower of sleet. At first, the noise from the cars along the road intruded on our privacy, but as we moved further back into the woods, the rush of the flooding river and the rising wind swallowed up highway sounds.

Much of the snow of the past week had melted. The land was a patchy gray and black, brown and deep green. Even after the recent record-low temperatures, chickweed was still bright, and garlic mustard, aster, henbit, wild strawberry, ground ivy, and sweet rocket leaves pushed out through the ice.

Deer tracks were visible in what was left of the snow. They were the only tracks I saw. Buttercup seemed not to notice them, preferred to romp and frisk, bite at sticks, climb over the stumps of fallen trees.

The water was as high as I'd ever seen it. Usually clear and shallow, it was deep and fast and full of mud after two days of rain and melting snow. Buttercup was nervous at its power, walked to the riverbank, then scampered back to me shaking, excited and afraid.

I walked with her, thinking how low this same river had been in the drought of 1988, how it had seemed so vulnerable and ephemeral then, how the fish had gathered in the deeper pools, huddled together against the increasing warmth and stagnation of the current and the mysterious withdrawal of the earth's life force.

Today, there was none of that old fragility, and Wendell Berry's poem on the second coming of the wilderness ran through my mind. I was standing, I imagined, in front of what Berry called "a resurrection of the wild."

This flood was like a sudden sweeping memory of a massive waterway 15,000 years ago when humans were just beginning to hunt in the newly-formed hills and when this excess would have been only low tide of that ancient global warming, the collapse of the ice age filling the hollows with snowmelt.

I wondered if the flood might also be a prophesy of this place 15,000 years from now, the valley filling again in the long storms of another climate, the river rising to cleanse the land of all our impurities, purging itself of our waste. Our words and structures would have disappeared by then, those people who might remain alive having no more knowledge of us than I of the fur-clad hunters and their wolf-dogs who tracked the ancestors of today's deer, men and women who stood in this same place as Buttercup and I and who wondered what might someday come to pass..

2001: Aconites at Susi's fully emerged with fat golden buds. At school, worms had been driven out of the ground by last night's rain, were stranded and frozen on the parking lot.

2002: First cardinal at 6:57. Skunk killed last night along Dayton-Yellow Springs Road.

2005: A flock of juncos was feeding around the woodpile this afternoon. Two sparrows were working on a nest in the birdhouse hanging on the west wall.

2006: This morning at 7:30, Bella and I walked through the Stafford-High Street alley. Cardinals were in full song, and I saw a large clump of aconites fully emerged and budded. The sky was dappled with clouds and pale blue sky, and the breeze was warm from the south. Two purple buds have appeared on the east garden snow crocus, but they did not open today.

2008: Cardinals and crows heard at 7:15. When I walked Bella through the alley, cardinals were singing throughout the neighborhood. And Dawn Shovar wrote: "We live straight west of Indianapolis, almost to the Illinois line, and on Saturday, the 16th, there were 5 buzzards sunning themselves on a hill along the roadside. I was glad to see them, but have not seen any redwings or robins yet. They can't be far behind, but are about two weeks late. They must have known this cold weather was coming. The chickens have finally started laying. There are some young hens who have not found the nesting boxes yet, so gathering eggs is like having an Easter egg hunt in the hay every evening. Sometimes one egg, sometimes four!"

2009: A cardinal sang at 7:03 this morning. Raw cold throughout the day, northeast wind. Judy wrote from Goshen, Indiana: "For the first time this year, heard the cardinals in full cry. I've heard a few tentative peeps now and then, but nothing like this morning. Hopeful!"

2011: Cardinal at 7:10 this morning, thaw deepening. More cardinals after sunrise and a red-winged blackbird-like song in the front honeysuckles.

2012: Cardinal singing after 9:00 a.m., soft rain, mild; more and more snowdrops are tall now and emerging from their sheaths. On my walk with Bella an hour later, I was surrounded by birdsong - cardinals, titmice, jays, doves, sparrows. The aconites in the alley are fat and yellow, their buds keeping back their pollen but still lighting up the ground with their globes. Buzzards circling and swooping over the south end of town - as they have done throughout the winter. They used to be a sign of spring; now they are fixtures of the cold, as well.

2014: Michele from Flying Mouse Farm said they were starting to collect sap today, about a week later than last year.

2016: First cardinal heard at 7:09 this morning. In the thaw, dark, open water spreads across the pond. Jill and I listened to crows and cardinals and doves, watched a large skunk lope across High Street when we walked at 7:30.

2017: I walked out the door at 7:00: A cardinal beyond Dayton Street called to greet me.

2018: Alabama/Tennessee line south to Panama City Beach. One early forsythia bush, some white clover and a dandelion at a rest stop half-way to Birmingham, and then after Birmingham, Middle Spring began to emerge with daffodils and plum blossoms, and then after Montgomery into northern Florida: pink magnolias (strong but starting to lose petals near the Gulf), red quince and one magnificent early redbud. Just a few observations, parts standing for the whole.

2019: First doves of the year heard about 8:00 a.m. this morning.

2020: Blue jay bell call, second day in a row, doves strong throughout my walk, a few cardinals.

2021: Finally the sun emerges after a week of clouds and snow. But below-zero temperatures forecast for tonight, six inches of new snow over the near foot of old. I got my car stuck in the driveway for the first time in over 40 years!

2022: Emily Foubert writes: "Titmice, chickadees, white throated sparrows, song sparrows, blue birds, eastern towhees, and white breasted nuthatches were all singing this morning, with woodpeckers drumming (their 'song')."

Journal

The exact end of winter came well before the most recent thaws, arriving unseen in the coldest weeks of the year when the March and April bulbs followed their own subterranean schedules and pushed up beneath the snow.

The cardinals, titmice and doves noted the temporal shift, even though the weather was harsh and the landscape white. While the sun and birds are already well on their way to equinox, however, the vegetation that now appears across local yards and gardens has changed little in the past weeks; it easily becomes a definition of the fulcrum that balances winter on one side and spring on the other.

Walking through town on Valentine's Day, I found that some daffodils were two inches high, and a few tulips and hyacinths were up at least an inch. Snowdrops, snow crocus and aconite were ready to bloom. Lilac buds were swollen, fat green and gold. Even on the old pussy willow branches, a few catkins were cracking. Garlic mustard, wild mallow and henbit were growing new leaves. A monarda patch showed half-inch foliage. Chickweed, wild strawberry, celandine, wild onion, hollyhock, sweet William, lamb's ear, lungwort, dandelion, motherwort, and great mullein had remained intact from fall and were waiting for a little more sun.

The beauty of a seasonal inventory is that there is never a correct number of things to find. Spring is as much a state of mind as a state of nature. The end of winter always appears in the eye of the beholder. Critical mass for the arrival of spring rests less on the total quantity of observations than on one crucial scent or sight or sound that tips the scales of private time. Each person encounters that pivotal event at a different moment and in a different way. Whenever that realization does occur, then the entire scaffolding of the old year collapses and the pieces of the new year take on meaning as they come together.

Simple attention to the details of nature, as always, helped me keep in sight both my center and my life's destination and purpose, which was to live skillfully and mindfully each step of the journey.

Stephen Altschuler

February 17th
The 48th Day of the Year

The advance of spring is neither logical nor linear. Spring does not always obey the measurements of the Sun, sometimes arrives all at once, sometimes hardly comes at all. And, like all seasons, it is evocative of different years, blending and separating, transporting the observer back a decade or a half century, teaching that nothing belongs where it seems to belong but that everything is welded together in repetition.

Leon Quel

Sunrise/set: 7:26/6:13
Day's Length: 10 hours 47 minutes
Average High/Low: 38/22
Average Temperature: 30
Record High: 70 – 1911
Record Low: - 11 – 1979

Weather

Seventy-five percent of the time, highs rise above freezing, making the typical temperature for this date the second warmest so far in the year. Sixties come five percent of the days, 50s occur 20 percent of the time, 40s twenty-five percent of the time, 30s thirty percent of the time, 20s fifteen percent, teens just five percent. Clouds continue to be the rule as blue sky appears just 40 percent of the days. The chances of rain: 25 percent, for snow: five to ten percent. Below-zero mornings come once in 15 years today, tomorrow and the 20th.

Natural Calendar

This week of February brings more substance to the natural history of the year, an increase in the number of flower, foliage, insect and bird sightings and birdcalls, a weightier accumulation of change than that of last week. That accumulation contributes a little more to the seasonal heritage of each region, adds to the composite of time that helps to define the cycles of passage. What happens along the 40th Parallel in one village is repeated in

115

countless others clustered along that marker, reveals what has already happened in Tennessee, forecasts the future for Wisconsin.

1983: First bee of the year seen today.

1985: First fly of the year seen today sitting on the snow. More opossums hit on the backroad to Wilberforce overnight.

1986: At the Covered Bridge: ducks on the river, paired.

1988: New moon, temperature 45 degrees, fishing at Sycamore Hole. River high from snowmelt, muddy, one chub, one shiner in more than an hour.

1989: More opossums killed on the road to Wilberforce. A raccoon yesterday.

1990: Some winter wheat fields are all green after the warmest, wettest January and February in history.

1993: The day after nine inches of snow, with the wind coming up now as the cold moves in (expecting a low of zero tonight), flurries, clouds and sun, no prospect of warm weather for days: but the first flock of robins arrived at Wilberforce. On a day when I am questioning my decisions and words, the robins remind me it's all right to do stupid things and to take too many risks.

1994: Doves heard at 2:00 this afternoon, the first time this year. Did they wait for this thaw?

1999: Pansy with a bud by the pond. Pussy willows opening. Dove heard at noon.

2000: Tufted titmouse drinking at the fountain this morning. And as I watched him, a robin came and settled in the quince bush to watch. No doves yet that I've heard.

2002: First cardinal at 6:58 a.m.

2005: The orange sun rising from the northeast corner of the Danielson's house at 7:40, the surrounding sky streaked gold and gray.

2006: Hard wind, thunder and lightning last night. Today, the cold has settled in, the wind still fairly strong. The snowdrops droop, and the snow crocus pull in.

2008: Tat called again from Wisconsin. They are expecting another foot of snow today – after hard rain and icing. Something like 84 inches so far in the year. In Yellow Springs, it is 50 degrees and cloudy, more rain coming today, but no snow. Jeanie and I smelled a skunk somewhere out on the freeway as we drove home from a concert in Dayton.

2009: Crisp and clear this morning, fourth-quarter moon halfway up in the east at 6:00. As I walked Bella in the alley, I heard the warble of a starling somewhere toward the center of town.

2011: The thaw continues, another day in the 60s, all the snow finally gone. The snowdrops are up, buds showing – they hadn't appeared in the New Year's Eve thaw. Daffodil spears have pushed an inch through the Osage leaves that were left in the garden. Foliage is emerging from one primrose plant by the redbud tree. Many of the Lenten rose stalks were broken by the ice storm of a few weeks ago, but the buds show under the drooping stems. Pussy willows are all half emerged. A baby skunk reported run down on the back road. Hard southwest wind this evening.

2012: Cardinals at 7:03 this morning, the earliest I've heard them this year, waning moon up in the southeast, reflected in the pond, sky before-dawn blue. Many many more daffodil buds in the north garden now, and the crocus along the south wall and the aconites in the alley are ready to bloom. Doves calling near midday. By 1:00 p.m. the snowdrop petals opened wide in the east garden, and the violet crocus (and one yellow one) were blooming along the south garden, and I found tulip and daylily foliage, too, up two to three inches. Then at about 2:00, Casey called: "I've got honeybees all over the aconites!" he said. "There's a lot of bees there." His aconites were clearly in full bloom.

2013: Reports from Wisconsin: almost a foot of snow on the ground in Madison. Here in southwestern Ohio, there is only a dusting of snow, but the progress of last week has retreated. One violet crocus is keeping its bud tight; the snowdrops have pulled back in. Pussy willows are still half open. Two days ago, I broke a silver maple branch from a tree near Ellis Pond, put it in water, and it opened yesterday morning.

One of the hellebores in the south garden is fully budded, one white flower open all the way. When I went out side at 7:00 this morning, a cardinal was in full song, the basic rule-of-thumb of cardinals singing at 7:00 on Cross-Quarter Day holding for another year. During the day, grackles visit the feeders (only arriving last week).

2014: The first skunk smell of the year drifted into the greenhouse from the back yard this morning. Yesterday was the first day of the Early Spring thaw, rain and sleet throughout the afternoon, the pond surface darkening as the snow turned to slush.

2015: Below zero this morning, record cold moving down to Florida, no thaw in sight for the next week, the Early Spring pattern absent this year.

2016: Mild, cloudy, quiet: Cardinal at 6:55 this morning. Thaw on the way. Pond more than half open now. The pussy willows I have cut and brought indoors open a few every day. The cluster I cut and set out in a container at the front of the house also comes in, but more slowly. Walking with Jill: we listened to titmice and cardinals and blue jays, saw flocks of robins stripping crabapples in the Bill Duncan park. Before lunch, Mary Sue wrote to say that a woolly bear caterpillar with a big black marking was crawling around on her porch,

2017: By the pond, the first aconite opened up (the only one of a dozen bulbs I planted two years ago), and two white standard crocuses, and a few violet snow crocuses. All around the yard, a quiet surging of the ground, a rising of grasses and wild plants, stalks and leaves climbing through the leaf mulch.

2018: Panama City Beach to Cedar Key, Florida, clouds and sun and 73 degrees: Driving through Panhandle scrub country, occasional redbuds and pink magnolias getting old, some full azaleas, many red flowering maple trees, most likely, some black medic in a driveway, a few of the endangered six-petal white lilies (*atamasco* lilies) with thin, basil, spreading leaves, stalks about two feet high, in the roadsides, six-petal like star grass here and there, one blue spiderwort, yellow roses, white roses, red roses throughout the neighborhood.

Walking in Cedar Key: Some large winter cress is in full flower by the museum (more winter cress seen along the highway in the scrublands further north. Three small sorrel blossoms. One patch of violets full blooming. Bright yellow sulphur butterflies crossing the road now and then. Doves constantly calling throughout the day. Brown pelicans clustering at the dock at evening. In Ohio, snow and rain coming to Yellow Springs, ending a deep thaw.

2020: The month continues mild, my hellebores open all the way, snowdrops with full unopened buds, the first snow crocus foliage showing, daffodils at four inches, wild onions low but bushy, no peony stalks yet, but ditch lilies are showing a little in the north garden.

2021: The coldest morning of the year, two degrees below zero, much of the nation in a deep freeze, Texas intermittently without power, and a second winter storm on the way. But the small triangle-shaped flies (probably a variety of drain flies or *Psychodidae*) appeared in the bathroom and the greenhouse for the first time since the end of autumn. And after a midwinter pause, the greenhouse geraniums have begun to bloom again. They know about Early Spring. This afternoon Ann from Cedarville wrote to report a bald eagle sighting.

2023: Only about a dozen geese at Ellis Pond today.

Journal

Recently, I wrote an article for the almanack about a fly that hatched in my house on a sunny day, and with whom I made friends the next morning. She was the first fly of the new millennium, and I felt protective of her. She seemed, at the time, like some risen Christ, a miracle of life sprung from brown Ohio winter, an exuberant, buzzing promise of spring.

My maudlin Franciscanism faded, however, as her brothers and sisters emerged from their hidden eggs. One fly I could befriend. Four pushy, loud and aggravating flies were something else again. And the spur of this great epiphany which took me from an idealized spring to a one of flesh and blood was the fly that ran into my cheek as I was working at the computer, ricocheted into my mug of tea, and screamed frantically for me to save her.

A week ago I would have rushed to pluck this comrade from certain death. Not so now. The affection I felt for the sacred first fly of the millennium was gone. Now I only saw the flies of everyday life, and they pledged not only the warmth and the clear skies of April, but hoards of other flies, and then Japanese beetles and carpenter bees and yellow jackets, cabbage worms and bean beetles, old enemies of mine, enemies who comforted me sometimes by their existence, but who were adversaries nonetheless.

I realized I would be lonely without them; they were, in a sense, guardian spirits, allies. But then too, I realized I had to set their limits. I, not they, had to be the God of this place. My heart hardened. I might have reached in and rescued last week's prophet. Instead, I let her drown right there beside my keyboard in the mug my Quaker sister had given me for Christmas.

The collector of observations can make sense of disparate times and happenings such as these, shaping a universe rich in events which never occur in isolation, a universe that is the sum of precedents and which is then enhanced and actually created by fractal repetition. And although not every seasonal event reoccurs at the same moment, meaning or sense in both human life and nature is dependent on the whole fabric of events that do reoccur.

The signs also enjoy power in their special season:
Summer comes with Gemini, Autumn with the Virgin,
Winter begins with Sagittarius, Spring with Pisces.

Manilius, *Astronomica*

Sunrise/set: 7:24/6:14
Day's Length: 10 hours 50 minutes
Average High/Low: 39/22
Average Temperature: 30
Record High: 66 – 2017
Record Low: - 9 – 1900

Weather

Between today and the 24th, there is a constant ten to 20 percent chance of an afternoon in the 60s - the first time that has happened since early December. Highs find 40 or above 70 percent of the time - making this, on average, the day with the warmest temperatures so far this year. A breakdown of those percentages: chances of 60s are 20 percent, of 50s another 20 percent, of 40s thirty percent, of 30s: ten percent, of 20s: ten percent, of teens ten percent. No sun is visible, however, 60 percent of February 18ths, and rain or snow falls four years in ten.

Natural Calendar

Today is Cross Quarter Day: the Sun reaches halfway to equinox. It enters Pisces at the same time, marking the astronomical border of the season of Early Spring, a six-week period of changeable conditions infiltrated ever so slowly by warmer and warmer temperatures that finally bring the maples and the early bulbs to bloom.

The night has shortened by 90 minutes through the space of the last 60 days, and the speed of the change reaches real spring levels along the 40th Parallel, the remaining gain of 70 minutes occurring between February 18 and equinox. The sun, which took 60 days to travel the first half of the way to equinox, suddenly doubles its speed, completing the second half of the journey in only 32 days.

On the star clock of the night, the Big Dipper, which lay due east of Polaris at 10:00 p.m. in late December, now intrudes deep overhead, well into the southeast. Orion, which filled the eastern sky before midnight at solstice, has shifted far into the southwest. Procyon is now the brightest star in the high south, not Sirius.

Weather statistics follow the sun and the stars. The average temperature of 26 degrees, which held through most of January, has climbed four degrees in the past 20 days. In the next four weeks, the average reaches its full springtime stride of one degree every three days, coming up 11 degrees to 41 by equinox.

These numbers and all of the others favor April over January. The February 15th cold front was the last of winter's 15 major high-pressure systems. From now on, the thaws, which often begin with highs in the 50s near Groundhog Day, steadily build momentum, the Early Spring thaws of February 18th, February 22nd, March 1st, March 5th, March 11th, and March 25th pushing and pushing until the full tide of wildflowers moves across the land.

The Robin Chorus

The earliest dates I have for the beginning of the robin chorus: February 20 in 2018, February 21 in 2023, February 22 in 2017, March 2 in 2011, March 3 in 2004, March 4 in 2020, March 7 in 2012, March 9 in 2013 and 2021, March 10 in 2010, March 15 in 2008, March 16 in 2009 and 2019, March 17 in 2003 and 2005.

Daybook

1983: Pussy willows pushing out from their red hulls. First peony stalks come through the mulch.

1984: Red-winged blackbird seen today at Jacoby swamp. The first maples flowering. Starlings were mating across from Sycamore Hole. Peonies came up today. The red quince at the northeast corner of the yard had one bud open.

1985: First cardinal sings at 6:58 a.m. At Mill Habitat: six inches of snow on the ground, river still frozen. So quiet, no birds except the rattle of a woodpecker up the hill toward John Bryant Park. Came across half-inch long insects walking on top of the snow, black, shaped like earwigs with a pincer type tail, like tiny walking sticks.

1986: First cardinal sings at 7:04 a.m. Winter wheat starting to turn green. Some grass growing a little. Poppies standing up strong. Crocus leaves, some three inches.

1987: Starlings mating at Wilberforce.

1988: First cardinal sings at 7:00 a.m. sharp.

1989: Four geese were scouting the river at the mill dam, and a muskrat was swimming against the current towards Lizard Tail Bend. Crows flew over. A flicker came to the back yard, and I saw another in the woods. Some peony stems are up.

1990: At South Glen, the river brown and high, chickweed growing back, a few honeysuckle bushes leafed out, others with bright green buds, mock orange the same. The yard has one pansy open, and a daffodil with a bud, two snowdrops with buds, and pussy willows are open like in the first or second week of March. Robins are common. The first rhubarb has not only unraveled, it has a red stalk four inches long. Peonies are up an inch under the mulch.

1991: Madison, Wisconsin:. There were crane flies and a small moth at the front porch light.

1992: One skunk, two opossums run over last night along the eight-mile road to school.

1993: Flock of juncos seen along Wilberforce-Clifton this morning, first flock seen this year. Then sparrows or some other similar birds feeding by the road, one almost hitting the windshield as I pass by. Eight hours later, the same sequence: another flock of juncos migrating, another sparrow almost killed against the car. In the office, the fly that emerged a few days ago is still trying to get out to snow and temperature in the teens, a forlorn robin outside in the ginkgo, feathers puffed out, waiting for him.

1994: Doves calling near dawn.

1999: Purple crocus opens today. The first golden crocus flower fades.

2002: First cardinal sings at 6:53 a.m.

2004: Margaret Lacy, a *News* reader from Richmond, Indiana wrote, "I saw a pair of doves courting on February 11, but I never heard a call till February 18."

2008: This evening about six o'clock, there was a snow burst that lasted maybe half an hour and spread over an inch of snow on the ground. I heard thunder as I was making a fire, and then Rick Donahoe called from over on Wright Street. He had been outside getting wood, and suddenly a huge bright light flashed above him, "a ball of light that flashed through the snow, sort of a halo in the middle of the blizzard. I didn't know what to think, and then a big clap of thunder sort of rolled through the snow. I wasn't sure the light was lightning until I heard the thunder."

2009: Mild and light rain, foliage of dandelion, celandine, chickweed growing around the yard. At 9:30 this morning, the back trees were filled with a great flock of s, blackbirds and a few starlings. This is the first of the migrations for the Shining Grackle Moon to reach Yellow Springs. At 3:30 this afternoon, Casey called with "big news": A flock of several dozen buzzards had arrived and was heading toward their regular roost along President Street.

2010: Over a foot of snow on the ground, with no melting in sight. The ground has been covered since the end of the Groundhog Day thaw. A cardinal sang at 7:50 this morning, and then again about 8:45 – the only audible motion toward spring.

2011: Warm in the 50s this morning. I heard the first cardinal at

7:05, and grackles, the first of 2011, were at the feeder by 7:45. Most of the ice at Ellis Pond has disappeared now, although Casey's ponds are still frozen. At John Bryan Park, a few violet hepatica leaves were visible, surrounded by leaves. The river was high from snowmelt. Three buzzards scouting. Wind still strong.

2012: Thin crescent moon in the southeast before dawn. Clear, temperature near freezing. Geese at 7:04, crows at 7:05, cardinals far off at 7:07. The aconites in the alley and a few on Stafford Street were open at 10:00. Throughout my walk, raucous blue jays, a red-bellied woodpecker, a pileated or a flicker, titmice, doves, cardinals, sparrows, full Early Spring song.

2013: Departing Yellow Springs for Oregon at 6:57 this morning: A cardinal sang just as I was getting into the car, half an hour before sunrise. A perfect dawn of cirrus and contrails, pink and gold and peach and powder-blue, streaked and swirling, brightening to a pure, clear yellow sun, and then a long morning of mackerel skies and a violet blue horizon south ahead of me, the east wind strong. The roadsides were a wintry brown throughout southern Ohio and northern Kentucky, finally breaking into sudden bloom with banks of daffodils near Bowling Green, Kentucky, and then fields of bright green winter grains.

An hour west of Nashville, red maples started to bloom, gradually gaining momentum until the tree line approaching Memphis was full of red and orange and silver from the flowers. At the Arkansas border: Red quince and forsythia were in full bloom, lanky ground ivy and bittercress, a few bluets. The sky turned dark as I drove through western Tennessee, the wind gusting, and then rain coming in bursts. But the buzzards, which had appeared along the Ohio River and stayed with me throughout the day, soared and zoomed across the sky in spite of, and maybe because of ,the hard wind, and near Memphis, great murmurations of starlings played in the storm, no mind to the lightning strikes all around as I approached Little Rock.

2014: Only scattered pussy willows open by the sidewalk so far this year, puffs white against the blue sky.

2016: Still, mostly clear morning, rose and a glowing gray-blue, upper 20s: the first High Street cardinal sang at 6:53, the first dove at 6:59, the first song sparrow at 7:00. Around 9:00, I saw a grackle at the feeder, the first grackle I've seen this winter.

2017: At the beginning of an Early Spring warm spell: Several daffodils budded, their foliage up to eight inches; day lily leaves three inches; hellebores and snowdrops and snow crocuses all early full bloom; squill leaves complete; pussy willow about half emerged; more aconites coming in; tulips and hyacinths and even a couple of peony shoots three inches.

2018: Cedar Key, Florida: In a walk along the old railroad path, I was interested to find that deciduous shrubs and trees had not begun to show any type of growth. Only the red maples are blooming here. Osprey nesting early this year, most birds mating from March through June, according to the boat guide.

2019: Leslie and her husband, Marc, stopped by when I was at the shop today, and they told me that they had just seen a great flock of grackles and red-winged blackbirds arrive in town, landing all about their property on Talus Drive. Leslie also said she found an aconite half open in her compost pile. At Ellis Pond, the geese were out in the soybean field west of the water, still hundreds, loud and coming and going. Tonight as I walked down High Street, geese were crying out in the distance.

2020: Chris Walker reports the first red-winged blackbird singing at his farm north of town.

2021: Deep freeze continues with highs only in the low 20s and flurries through the day.

2023: Very similar to 2017, with the addition of gold appearing on two daffodil buds. So far the month's average is 38.5 degrees.

Journal
Aboriginal Creation myths tell of the legendary totemic beings who had wandered over the continent in the Dreamtime, singing out the

name of everything that crossed their path – birds, animals, plants, rocks, waterholes – and so singing the world into existence.

Bruce Chatwin, *The Songlines*

The shift in weather that multiplies the signs of spring usually takes place within a week of Cross Quarter Day (February 18), the day on which the Sun reaches halfway to spring equinox. Even if the winter is gray and long, solar progress leaves a trail of familiar signs.

The year takes on its character from those signs, or what anthropologist Keith Basso calls "mnemonic pegs." A person might use such pegs, formed by objects or events, like sprouting crocuses or singing birds, to formulate a "topogeny," a listing of phenomena that creates maps or paths.

In his *On Trails*, Robert Moore explains that topogeny "is the summoning, in the mind's eye, of a mental landscape...." Like the technique of singing the names of landmarks for navigation, used by the aboriginal inhabitants of Australia and described by Bruce Chatwin in *The Songlines*, the naming of flora and fauna, in context, becomes a sequence of markers with which one can plot time and place.

In the coldest springs, it often seem I am lost in a monotony of snow and rain and gray, but then if I walk about and look closely, I might see pussy willows pushing out from their ruddy hulls, the first red-winged blackbirds at the Glass Farm, early robins eating crabapples, geese pairing near Ellis Pond, a few budded snowdrops, maybe the earliest violet crocus or yellow aconite in bloom.

If I keep walking and hear cardinals and titmice and blue jays calling, and then if I collect signs for just a few days, I will have the map. I will know exactly where I am and can't possibly lose my way to equinox.

February 19th
The 50th Day of the Year

Great rumors are afloat in the air of a great and coming change. We are eager for Winter to be gone.... But he will not abdicate without a struggle. Day after day he rallies his scattered forces, and night after night pitches his white tents on the hills, and would fain regain his lost ground; but the young prince in every encounter prevails. Slowly and reluctantly the gray old hero retreats up the mountain, until finally the south rain comes in earnest, and in a night he is dead.

John Burroughs

Sunrise/set: 7:23/6:15
Day's Length: 10 hours 52 minutes
Average High/Low: 39/22
Average Temperature: 31
Record High: 70 – 1939, 71 – 2018
Record Low: - 11 – 1910

Weather

Chances of a highs in the 60s or even 70s are ten percent today. There is a 25 percent chance of 50s, thirty-five percent of 40s, twenty percent of 30s, and just ten percent of 20s. Rain falls 20 percent of the years, snow five percent. This is the last morning of the month on which a below-zero reading is likely.

Natural Calendar

Frequency becomes a new marker of change as February unravels. The first stage in the progress of spring is the sighting of "firsts": first bluebird, first robin, and so forth. After that, quantity counts as much as much as novelty. The number of robins, the number of blackbirds, the number of blooming bulbs, the number of pussy willow catkins emerging take on more and more importance until the next stage of the year arrives, the stage at which all the old first creatures and events are commonplace and give way to new firsts and new quantities.

1983: Second bee of the year. At Jacoby swamp, skunk cabbage burned by the cold but blooming. Blackbirds at the swamp in the distance, sounded like redwings.

1984: First robin on High Street.

1987: Pussy willows brought in yesterday, opened almost completely by this afternoon.

1988: First opossum killed along Grinnell Road.

1989: First blue jay of the year heard this morning. Cardinals sing by 6:56 a.m., doves by 8:15.

1992: One worm seen crossing the sidewalk in the rain.

1993: Deep freeze continues, nine inches of snow on the ground. Early Spring is late for the first time in years. No prospect for change in sight. But at 7:06 a.m., I heard the first cardinal. At 4:30 this afternoon along Wilberforce-Clifton, a flock of cardinals was heading north. Up the hill, more juncos, more sparrows, and a couple of robins.

1994: Temperature up into the 60s this morning. Bright sun. I rode my bike downtown without a jacket. Juncos still at the bird feeder. One of the goldfinches seemed brighter, more yellow.

1998: Morning birds are definitely louder now. Crows more boisterous.

1999: Doves were singing at 9:00 a.m.

2000: To Springfield at 7:00 this morning. Parked at St. John's, I watched the crows move north for half an hour. No more seen during the day, but coming home after work, another flock was flying east to west near the dairy.

2001: Snow crocus, light purple on Elm Street. Pear leaves finally down. First fly at school.

2002: This year's first flock of robins seen on campus in Columbus.

2004: A cardinal was singing at 7:00 a.m., the morning mild and the sky pale pink and violet. This evening, Bob Huston told me that his mother had seen a yellow aconite – only one – blooming this afternoon. That would be the first flower noted in 2004.

2005: Roadkills gradually increasing through the month: skunks, raccoons, opossums.

2008: After last night's snowburst and wind, today is bitter cold. A cardinal was singing at 7:30, though, and the crows were calling.

2010: Very cold and sunny, a foot of snow on the ground, but a skunk was out around the house (odor really strong in the bedroom) before daylight this morning, and a cardinal sang at 7:00 for the first time that early this year.

2011: I was standing out side for a while this morning, heard the first faint cardinals at 6:55, then doves a few minutes later, then a flock of crows went over at 7:00, and then cardinals and sparrows moved in from the honeysuckles to the feeders. By late afternoon, several snowdrop flowers had emerged from their stalks and we ready to open.

Liz wrote: "Just a quick note to let you know that I saw two bluebirds at Ellis Pond this morning! yaay spring!" And Loretta Benner wrote: "I want to tell you an amazing thing from yesterday morning as I was eating my breakfast in the kitchen. Our table is in front of double windows overlooking the front down to the road. Well, I kept seeing all of these birds hopping over the lawn and they were more near the creek. I kept watching as they kept coming up closer to the house. Suddenly I thought those look like robins! As they kept hopping they kept coming from the right side facing the house. I could see them closer up and lo and behold they were robins! I started counting all the way to 22 but they were still coming more and more and closer making a huge flock.

God must have wanted me to perk up as it sure did make my day! Never in my life did I ever see such a flock of robins! Robins....the harbinger of spring! A wonderful experience I won't ever forget!"

Tonight, I talked with Rosemary and Jim. Rosemary's aconites had bloomed two days ago, and this afternoon she and Jim had seen a cloud of buzzards, "hundreds of buzzards" circling the southeast part of the village.

2012: Crows, then a cardinal within a few seconds at 6:57 this morning. I was waiting outside for them. Blue-eyes seen blooming by the side of Limestone Street this morning, the first time I've seen them so early. In the south garden, hellebores continue to bloom, their flowering consistent through the month. The small flock of starlings continues at the feeders, a late-winter/Early Spring pattern.

2013: On the road: Another perfect start to the day, clear sky, a dawn layered in deep reds and oranges and yellows up into pale turquoise. I drove west from Little Rock into Oklahoma to Amarillo, Texas. Yesterday's trip south brought me into Yellow Springs April, but today's miles held the season steady for a while, and then regressed as I climbed into the high plains. Skunks were the surest sign of spring along the way. I counted and smelled nine skunk roadkills. Buzzards still accompanied me, but most of them flying higher than they did yesterday. A few small flocks of starlings, but no swarming murmurations.

And even though there were few flowers open, I did see several reckless winter cress plants by the side of the road in Oklahoma City, full bloom, waving in the hard wind and all the traffic. In western Oklahoma, clover foliage was starting to grow into clumps, and I saw one patch of purple ground ivy growing in grass almost long enough to cut – all signs of April further north along the 40th Parallel. The sky, so pure and empty through the morning, gathered vast sweeping cirrus through the afternoon until once again by evening a storm was forming. Tomorrow brings rain in Texas and New Mexico, snow across the region I just crossed yesterday. And maybe snow at Flagstaff, where I hope to end up tomorrow.

2014: When I went out for wood at 5:35 this morning, I could hear a screech owl in the back woods. Walking Bella before dawn, third quarter moon in the southwest, temperature just about at freezing, standing water on the sidewalk, some ice on the street: I heard the first cardinal at 6:52 along Limestone Street, crows when I was on Stafford Street at 6:59. When I went out into the back yard at 7:05, a song sparrow, the first I've heard this spring, was singing.

2016: Steady south wind all day bringing highs in the 50s and Early Spring. Deep scarlet peony stalks pushed up a little through the leaf mulch. The snowdrops that had bloomed, then were covered by the snow, perked up, their petals opening again.

2017: Heavy fog, 44 degrees, in the second day of an Early Spring heat wave: Cardinals – the whole neighborhood, it seemed – at 6:55 a.m., then doves at 6:58, a song sparrow across the street, crows from the north end of town at 7:02.

2018: Cedar Key to Shell Mound and Manatee Springs: At Manatee Springs State Park along the Suwannee River, the high tree line is greening, and among the cypress knees that shadow the clear springs, I found the first shrubs and trees starting to leaf. Once the scrub area was softened by a greater variety of species, more giving soil, spring came more quickly. In Yellow Springs, a new heat wave brings a record high of 71 degrees, just three degrees cooler than here in northwestern Florida.

2019: Sunny, crisp and frosty at 15 degrees this morning. In the Stafford Street alley, the very first cardinal at 6:56, crows at 6:59, doves at 7:04. Birds at or before 7:00 a.m. are a clear marker for Early Spring. A red-tailed hawk screeched as it flew overhead around 7:45, and then a blue jay's bell call. The geese are back at their field across from Ellis Pond, several chasing each other across the flooded area near the bike path. When I went to read my almanacks, Brad Roof told me he had seen another bald eagle near Kaiser Lake.

2020: Leslie reports a coyote yipping in the field south of Talus

Drive around 3:00 a.m.

2023: Sun and mild and wind. Song sparrows singing. One grackle. More tulips coming up. More daffodils budding. More tiny sprouts appearing. Jeff says: "Doves, robins, cardinals, crocuses." On he way home from a walk, Jill and I saw a honeybee in the mulch. When I went outside to the studio at 6:00, I heard robins all around the yard. Before bed, note from Chris Welker: "First harbinger of spring is popping up in our woods." Finally, a complement to my 2020 entry: reports of coyotes north and west of town.

To deliver oneself up, to hand oneself over, entrust oneself completely to the silence of a wide landscape of woods and hills, or sea, or desert; to sit still while the sun comes up over the land and fills its silences with light. To pray and work in the morning and to labor and rest in the afternoon, and to sit again in meditation in the evening when the night falls upon that land and when the silence fills itself with darkness and with stars. This is a true and special vocation.

Thomas Merton, *Thoughts in Solitude*

And what if all of animated nature
Be but organic harps diversely framed,
That tremble into thought, as o'er them sweeps
Plastic and vast, one intellectual breeze,
At once the Soul of each, and God of all?

Samuel Taylor Coleridge

Sunrise/set: 7:22/6:17
Day's Length: 10 hours 55 minutes
Average High/Low: 39/22
Average Temperature: 31
Record High: 69 – 1891, 69 – 2016, 77 – 2018
Record Low: - 15 – 1885

Weather

Today's statistics are even more promising than those of the 18th: five percent of February 20ths are in the 60s or 70s, 20 percent in the 50s, fifty-five percent in the 40s, twenty percent in the 30s. The sun shines half the time, and the chances of precipitation are the lowest of the month (just 20 percent). Below-zero temperatures are rarely recorded between now and the end of February.

Natural Calendar

Mountain bluebirds return to Yellowstone. Bald eagles lay eggs. Ravens pair up for spring, frolicking as they court. Snow midges appear as the weather becomes milder along the mountain streams; they provide early food for birds and fish, which become more active as equinox approaches. All across the deserts of the Southwest, wildflower season has begun in wetter years, with large white desert lilies in full bloom and bright purple sand verbena blossoming where moisture is adequate.

Farmers plant their sweet corn along the Gulf coast. Fields of daffodils are open in southern Georgia, and bee season has started there; honeybees and bumble bees collect pollen from dandelions, yellow-flowered wild radishes, red maples, blue toadflax, white clover and mouse-eared chickweed. Azaleas are blooming in Alabama. In the lowlands of Mississippi, swamp buttercups, violets and black medic are open.

The Stars

The pointers of the Big Dipper are positioned northwest/southwest about ten o'clock tonight. When they point north-south at that time of night in a few weeks, Middle Spring will spread across the nation's midsection.

Daybook

1983: First new strawberry leaves came out today.

1984: First new strawberry leaves found today.

1987: Clear and 24 degrees. Cardinal sings at 6:45 a.m.

1989: Blue jays heard again, stronger today.

1991: Snowdrops have been budding in the south garden for about a week. Aconites are up, red stems awkward, gangly like birds just out of the egg, necks wobbly, looking to the ground. Some daffodils up six inches in the mulch. Rhubarb is continuing to unravel, and crocus foliage is taller. In the greenhouse, the tomatoes are still lush, still producing, some with full summer-size fruits. White flies strong, but under control. Mother-of-millions is still in bloom.

1994: Squirrels mating with wild acrobatics, leaping and frolicking in the back locusts this morning. Jane Morgan's snowdrops have bloomed within the past few days in spite of the cold. In the south garden, not a sign of mine.

1995: To Jekyll Island off the southern coast of Georgia. It was cold and cloudy when we left Yellow Springs, and the clouds stayed all the way to the island. Temperatures also remained fairly steady throughout the 840-mile trip, and our two days on the beach were rainy, with highs only in the 50s. We did find spring in spite of the cold. Buzzards were circling the Great Smoky Mountains, and miles of trees were budding between Knoxville and Asheville. Below Columbia, South Carolina, the first real sign of a new season visible from the moving car was growth on the wild onions (and on the way back, I found two swamp buttercups in full bloom at a rest area near Asheville).

The closer we came to Charleston, the larger the tree buds, and then by Savannah the trees were blooming, most of them an orange which turned to deep red by the time we got to Brunswick. Just before our turnoff to the island, I spotted a redbud in full flower. Then on Jekyll, there were azaleas and rhododendrons in early bloom, a few violets, some sprawling blackberry vines blossoming, plenty of black medic, and four or five small-flowered weeds I taped into the daybook but haven't identified yet. The great southern thistles, two and three feet in diameter, were starting to bud near the ocean. From all of this, it seems Jekyll Island is six to eight weeks ahead of Yellow Springs, about a hundred miles a week. Much different from my late January trip to this area in warm 1989, when things were actually ahead of where there are now in southern Georgia.

2000: Crows heard at 7:02 a.m.

2001: Doves calling at sunrise, first daylily spears up in the garden, pussy willows breaking out on the front shrub, golden crocus blooming in the south garden.

2004: Mike and I saw three rufus-sided towhees this morning in the South Glen. One of the males was courting; we surprised them in their ritual. Coming back along the river, we heard red-tailed hawks. Were they courting too?

2005: Snowdrops have reached full bloom in spite of the cool temperatures of the past week. More of the new snow crocus leaves have emerged, buds not far behind. The highs and lows are about average for this time of year, and the first part of the floral season complements the weather.

2009: The morning was sunny and cold, gathering high clouds, storm on the way. We left Yellow Springs in a hurry late in the afternoon, drove south to Louisville, the road brown and gray under overcast sky.

2010: Cold and gray this morning. A cardinal was singing in the honeysuckles when I walked out to get some wood at 7:20. The snow levels went down quite a bit yesterday, more branches emerging. More thawing today. Judy writes from northern Indiana: "The starlings are here! Coming back from grocery shopping, I saw a small flock in one of the trees on Meadow Ridge. This is the first I've seen. The cardinals are getting more assertive every morning, and perhaps I heard some starlings, too, this morning. Their squawks are so unattractive, I'm pretty sure it was they. Can't wait for spring, hope they brought some!! But day before yesterday, the air had that soft, pussy willow smell that gives one hope. I'm certainly ready."

2011: Cardinal heard at 6:58 this morning.

2012: Geese at 7:03, cardinals at 7:05, crows a few minutes later. And then steady cardinal song throughout the morning. I saw a Cooper's hawk in front of the Village Artisan store downtown when I was coming back from the radio station. Peter had just told me how he thought it was hawk season, a Cooper's hawk and a red-tailed hawk having come to his yard just in the past week.

2013: West from Amarillo, Texas into New Mexico and then to California: The sun once again rose at my back, and the sky was clear at first, then brought cirrus in late morning, and then all kinds of mixes in the afternoon, especially after I drove through Albuquerque and started the ascent to Flagstaff – when the benign sky and winds changed quickly, and the atmosphere became more turbulent. I entered a world of snow bursts and wind and miles of fogs and then of jagged, intermittent blue, a world of stratus-clouds, broken formations moving beside me, leading me on.

I remember a dark, shark-shaped cloud swimming across the cumulus and altostratus. The snow bursts continued through the mountains, turning into a real snowstorm as I approached Flagstaff. I was glad to get in to a motel, and the snow continued to blow on through the night.

2014: Skunk odor around the house when I got up this morning. Walked Bella early again, crows calling first, then cardinals about 6:50. A skunk surprised us in the Phillips Street alley, then ran off into the honeysuckles. Then at 7:40, the first thunderstorm of the year and a tremendous surge of rain and wind against the greenhouse windows, the strongest gust I've ever felt here.

2015: Almost ten below zero, clear, no wind: I went out with Bella at sunrise, cardinals singing all around us.

2016: Close to record high in the upper 60s today, lots of sun. One clump of purple snow crocus in bloom at the corner of Walnut and Elm Streets across from the school. At home, one violet snow crocus opened in the east garden near the flowering snowdrops, and a large cluster between bamboo stalks near the fishpond on the south side of the house. Returning from Beavercreek, I came upon a vast flock of blackbirds feeding in the fields.

2017: Heavy fog this morning, in the third day of a deep warm-up. As the sun burns away the fog, more violet snow crocus bloom by the south wall, and the clumps by the front gate, which receive less light, are flowering, too. I left the back screen door open this afternoon, and the first small mosquito came in to circle around me.

2018: Emily Foubert reported the robin chorus before dawn this morning, a day earlier than my record of last year. Also, she sent a photo of violet snow crocus blooming along the bike path. From Cedar Key to St. Augustine, more trees leafing, much more Jessamine throughout the drive, fallen live oak tree leaves common. This evening, a note from Chris Walker about a half hour north of Yellow Springs: "As I was walking out for Compline at about 8:00, I heard spring peepers. Also yesterday afternoon. I have seen no Harbinger of Spring or other early flowers in our woods yet, but saw a bunch of snowdrops in Urbana this evening

2020: The alley's chickadee calls "sweetee" as I pass by. At Ellis

Pond, the water is filled with what must be at least 400 Canadian geese.

2022: A note from Emily Foubert: "Heard my first killdeer calling in the fields at Agraria on Friday. And right now on my walk on Sunday evening, I hear red-winged blackbirds in the wet fields along the bike path close to where the little Miami crosses under Route 68."

2023: It seems the great flocks of geese have left. Only a handful left near Ellis Pond today.

In belonging to a landscape, one feels a rightness, at-homeness, a knitting of self and world. This condition of clarity and focus, this being fully present, is akin to what the Buddhists call mindfulness, what Christian contemplatives refer to as recollection, what Quakers call centering down.

Scott Russell Sanders

February 21st
The 52nd Day of the Year

Place is dynamic, equal parts geography and imagination; it is a complex intermingling and, ultimately, fusion of mind and landscape, so that neither is finally separable or meaningful without the other.

Kent C. Ryden

Sunrise/set: 7:20/6:18
Day's Length: 10 hours 58 minutes
Average High/Low: 40/23
Average Temperature: 31
Record High: 68 – 1930 /66 or higher – 2018
Record Low: - 12 – 1885

Weather

This is another mild, early-spring day in many years, with only a 25 percent chance of an afternoon high below 40 degrees. The full temperature breakdown: ten percent chance of a high in the 60s, twenty-five percent of 50s, forty percent of 40s, fifteen percent of 30s and just ten percent of 20s. Precipitation is likely, however: 50 percent of the years bring rain or snow. Clouds obscure the sun 65 percent of the time.

The Week Ahead

This is often Snowdrop Winter Week along the 40th Parallel, a time of meteorological ambivalence, promising spring then backsliding. First the warmth: The fifth major high pressure system of February comes through in the early days of the week, but it is typically the weakest front of the month. The 21st is usually mild, and the 22nd and 23rd are typically the very warmest days of the entire month. On those dates, for the first time since December 12th, there is at least a 20 percent chance of 60s, along with a 20 percent chance of 50s.

Then a step backward: Snowdrop Winter arrives around the 24th, often one of the windiest days of the month, and colder temperatures often return for up to 72 hours. While 50s and 60s each come five percent of the time, and 40s are recorded 35 to 40 percent of the years, highs only in the 20s or 30s occur the remaining 50 percent, and chances of a high in the teens appear for the last time this season. Snow falls 35 percent of the years on the 24th, and five years in ten on the 25th. But the 25th is also the last day in Early Spring that chances of snow get so high.

Natural Calendar

The final week of February brings the Season of Snowdrop Winter to the region, slowing the advance of Early Spring, but still allowing other seasons to continue. Even in cold Montana, Bald Eagle Egg Laying Season marks this time of year. Hear in the Midwest, Horned Owl Hatching Season closes Horned Owl Nesting Season.

Throughout Georgia, Bee Season follows Pollen Season as honeybees and carpenter bees collect pollen from dandelions, yellow-flowered wild radishes, red maples, blue toadflax, white clover and mouse-eared chickweed. Azaleas are blooming in Alabama. All across the Southwest, Desert Wildflower Season occurs whenever the rainfall allows. Throughout the Ohio Valley, Daffodil Budding Season spreads beside Early Dandelion Blooming Season and Silver Maple Blooming Season.

In Lake Erie, the Steelhead Salmon Run Season, which started in the fall, finally comes to a close. In Florida, Sweet Corn Season shows tall sprouts, as Rhododendron Blooming Season takes over southern Texas. Throughout the country, Horse Breeding Season begins on ranches as mares show signs of estrus in the lengthening days.

Along the 40th Parallel, the days now lengthen at the rate of 60 seconds every 160 minutes. Crows and doves and cardinals (and sometimes robins) are up by 6:45 in the morning. At 7:30, there is really a chorus of cardinals, blue jays, song sparrows, crows and titmice filling the landscape with sound.

As temperatures warm, sap runs in the maples, partial to new and full-moon times. Horned owlets hatch in the woods. And between the third week of February and the middle of March, sandhill cranes often pass through southwestern Ohio on their way north to nesting sites, and grackles join the starlings at feeders across the Lower Midwest. In the Platte River region of Nebraska, thousands of sandhills and snow geese gather for migration north.

Daybook

1984: Fern Albertson called: her first crocus bloomed. Saw Mrs. Dawson in the store, her crocus are blooming, too.

1985: Jane Morgan phoned at 4:15 this afternoon. Her snowdrops are open in the Vale: "Once the temperature got to the 40s," she told me, "and the ice melted around them, they flowered."

1988: Rivers flushed and muddy. Not even a nibble at Sycamore Hole.

1990: First calf seen in a field along Wilberforce-Clifton Road.

1991: Rivers high in the Glen and at Wilberforce.

1992: Snowdrops ready to bloom, aconite cracking, robins seen and heard migrating into South Glen. Silence of Late Winter completely gone.

1993: Eight inches of snow on the ground, the barometer at 29.48, still falling, gusts of wind and hard rain.

1994: Jeni says the trees are starting to leaf out in northern Florida.

1996: First dove heard this morning. Then a flock of robins came through Wilberforce at 12:30 this afternoon, the first sighting here.

2000: After five weeks of cold, with few days in the 40s, now the temperature rises to the 50s with sun. In the nearly frozen east garden, one purple snow crocus bud appeared. Two batches of snowdrops, the ones from Ruby, and four pussy willow catkins were showing.

2005: Jeanie tapped her maple trees at Antioch School. The sap was running, she said.

2006: Blue jay heard this morning.

2008: Low near zero this morning. Cardinals strong as I walked Bella through the snow around 9:30. In the backyard, the first song sparrow heard. Around noon, a mockingbird began feeding at the suet in the front yard. Tonight, more snow, the town quiet and white.

2009: Louisville, Kentucky to Pelham, south of Birmingham, Alabama. A very gradual greening of the landscape, especially below Bowling Green. Clumps of daffodils noticed below Nashville, about 370 miles southwest of Yellow Springs, then bright, low wheat fields glowing near the Alabama-Tennessee border. A few dandelions and many gil-over-ground at the Alabama welcome center. Between Huntsville and Birmingham, the first flowering plum trees, bringing us well into Lower Midwestern April as we reached about 500 miles from home.

2012: Cooler weather is keeping the snowdrops half open, the snow crocus and aconites just budding until the sun shines and then they open. The rate of advance has slowed after several days in the 30s; now, 40s are holding the steep progress of the past three weeks in check, but allowing a gentle stability in the swelling of the season.

2013: Flagstaff, Arizona to Fresno, California: I had been skeptical of the weather forecasts of blizzards and closed roads yesterday, but even though the big storm came through south of Flagstaff, the effects were relatively severe – something I did not respect until I started out this morning at 5:00. The roads were wet but clear in Flagstaff, but they deteriorated quickly as I drove west. Soon I was going along at about 45 mph, trying to stay in the tracks of the cars in front of me. The darkness impaired my vision, and it wasn't until maybe an hour later that the conditions got better.

As I drove west in the dark, the only light in the sky came from the southwest, a red glow that I imagined was from Los Angeles, 450 miles away. The sky eventually brightened, the icy roads gave way to clarity, and I made the descent through more snow bursts and gusts into the quiet and sunny Mojave Desert, an elegant respite from the bitter cold and treacherous snow of the mountains of Arizona.

The day brightened, and I could see solitary crows and pairs and small flocks of crows scavenging in the waysides. Sometimes I saw single crows sitting on fence posts like red-winged blackbirds in the North. There were no buzzards here, but I was surprised by two golden eagles feeding on a roadkill by the side of the freeway.

And the daylight too revealed the vast landscape for which I have no words. At home in Ohio, I live in a cramped and tiny habitat, enclosed by maples and oaks that close out the sky or reduce it to patches and glimpses, and I watch closely the stamens and pistils of the flowers that open through the year, but I have no vocabulary for the immensity of the West, the great stretches of open land, the hills so varied and distant (each one a landmark to those who live close by), the amazing fissures in the clouds (the clouds always big like the mountains) that came into focus as I drove down and west and south on roads that led as far as I could see and imagine.

Then finally out of the cold, I drove back into the April I had left in Oklahoma, even though the blooming plants I found were not the same as the ones there or at home. I came into an April of unknown and unnamed flowers, a landscape for which I had no language, in a place of countless foreign formations, of prickly and twisted growths and clumps of tough, sinewy fibers, stones that took the place of grass, tight, bold, scrubby, tough, thick-leaved defiant, persistent plants, roadsides full of yellow and purple blossoms, saying that winter was the true desert, not this paradise of sun and weeds of exceptional fortitude.

And it was too a land in which my friend Ruby would have discovered animal shapes everywhere. (When she took me out for a ride once, just before her 100th birthday, she kept asking me: "So what does that tree look like?" "What does that hill look like?" And when I invariably gave her the wrong answer, she would respond, "NO – it's a ….. Can't you see it?" And she would point and explain. And here, the choices and the options were infinite. I tried to respond to an imaginary Ruby, telling her that the hills looked like the mounds of behemoth, ancient moles or stones swept up and fashioned by the turbulent inland sea that once ebbed and flowed across these places. But I knew she would have seen so much more.

Leaving the Mojave behind, I drove up toward Bakersfield and then Fresno, deeper into Yellow Springs April. Cherry and plum and apple trees were just starting to flower, and beehives were set out in their orchards to pollinate the blossoms. Different varieties of cress, similar to the winter cress and the spring cress of the Midwest, were blooming, and the row crops were tall as my boot everywhere. Citrus orchards held their fruit, and the vineyards were budded.

2014: After a night of rain, most of the snow and ice has melted, and the yard is flooded. Skunk odor again around the house. Snowdrops have grown some under the snow, and tips of daffodils and crocus are just barely visible. The barometer just started to rise at dawn, and the wind shifted to the west. I heard no birds at first this morning, even though Bella and I came upon two skunks in the Phillips Street alley at 7:00. Ten minutes later, a cardinal was chipping and the song sparrow sang intermittently. Crows didn't call until 7:15. As the snow melted in the circle garden today, I found that daffodil foliage had pushed up even while the snow cover remained for weeks. The same thing in the front garden: crocus and snowdrops were not inhibited by the cold.

2016: A soft morning, 45 degrees and cloudy, windless. The first cardinal on High Street sang at 6:49. I heard the first dove at 6:54. Several geese flew over at 7:02. At a little after 9:00, Jonatha Wright sent a photo of a honeybee on an aconite, and when I was talking to Ann on the front porch, we watched a honeybee in one of my violet crocuses. Then at 11:00, Ed Oxley called to say he had honeybees in his "thousands of snowdrops" and aconites and crocuses. And when Jill and I walked down High Street after lunch: more clumps of violet crocuses, more honeybees!
From Arizona, Joe Stewart wrote: "The wildflowers are just starting. The last two weeks, the desert has begun to green up. Cactus flowers are not expected until late March or early April."

2017: Fourth day of a warm-up, 52 degrees before sunup. I went out about 6:30 listening for cardinals. A small tan moth flew away into the dooryard garden as I went down the steps. No birds until

6:47, and then I heard a robin whinny. Two minutes later, a robin singsong call, the first of the robin chorus for the year. The earliest I recorded it before was March 2nd of 2011. A grackle at the feeder before noon, the second I've seen so far, then a small flock early in the afternoon. At the Covered Bridge, skunk cabbage is red and stiff and open, no longer hidden in the grasses. Along the river, hemlock was bright and bushy, almost a foot high. On Walnut Street, a whole back yard full of violet crocuses. A few more violet crocuses at home, as well, and then the very first blue squill of the year in the southwest garden near the studio.

2018: Early this morning in Yellow Springs, the temperature was in the upper 60s, rain all day, more rain coming for the next three or four days. Judy reports flooding and a state of emergency, streets under water and the like, in Goshen and Elkhart, Indiana. Here in St. Augustine, very little new from the past week, except a few white violets in the graveyard near the Virgin de la Leche church. And the azaleas through the city are getting quite old, losing color and petals.

2019: Doves were calling when I went out the front door at 7:00 this morning, the eastern sky bright blue, the orange, waning, gibbous moon setting in the west. I heard crows about two minutes later, distant cardinals by 7:05. At Ellis Pond this noon, I listened to the recently arrived red-winged blackbirds whistling around me. Doves called steadily throughout the day.

2020: In 1978, when I moved to Yellow Springs and began to record random events in nature, some of my first notes were about Canadian geese flying over town. I didn't realize it at the time, but the numbers of Canadian geese had been dramatically reduced in the first half of the 20th century and were only beginning to increase in Ohio.

My friend Casey, who grew up in Yellow Springs, remembers that in the 1960s, people used to feed just a few geese at DeWine's Pond, and that ducks were more common than geese in the area. Since then, the goose flock has grown considerably, and in recent years, January and February bring hundreds of those birds to Ellis Pond and nearby pastures.

This past week, there were what I estimated to be around 400 geese gathered in and around the pond. It was the second day of a cold snap. The sun was bright, the blue sky deepening the color of the pond to indigo, the white breasts of the geese shining against their black feathers. It was, as my friend Ruby might have said, a sight to see.

Such a gathering is now a rite of village winter, and the departure in pairs a rite of village spring. Soon the great assembly will scatter for nesting throughout the region. Breeding takes place in March and April, and eggs hatch after about five or six weeks. Most chicks appear in late spring. Molting of the adults takes place in middle summer, but flocking does not begin again until late summer. By September, the calls and flights of the geese over Yellow Springs resume, and the gathering begins once more.

While some people may consider the Canadian goose a nuisance, the residents of Yellow Springs have been graced with an annual ritual that attests to the success of wildlife management as well as offers a gauge of the seasons and the still-vital natural world. (Written for the *Yellow Springs News*)

2021: Finally, thaw, highs in the middle 30s! And Chris wrote from his farm north of the village: "The buzzards are back!"

2022: First dove call heard this morning. The first day at 60 degrees. More daffodils are just barely emerging in the north and circle gardens. Red ladybugs (not the Asian variety) swarmed in Jill's back porch. And "Wowza! 120 red winged black birds in fields south of Xenia today. They're really moving!" writes Emily.

2023: Light wind, clouds, rain drops before daylight. Waiting for birds to sing before 7:00, I went inside for a little while, and when I came out at 7:05, I heard cardinals, Carolina wrens, song sparrows, doves and even sing-song calls of robins, the first of the robin chorus. In the morning sun, the first daffodil is opening.

To the natural philosopher there is no natural object unimportant or trifling...a soap bubble...an apple...a pebble...He walks in the midst of wonders.

John Herschel

February 22nd
The 53rd Day of the Year

The buzzing of a bee said that the frost was out at the edge of the marsh, that the sap was flowing....There had been other signs of the turn of the seasons: the faint odor of skunk in the air... And then in the distance could be heard the sound of a flock of blackbirds arriving, a rustling sound like the wind in the leaves of the cottonwood. The next night, the thunder cracked and the first rain of spring fell.

Paul Gruchow

Sunrise/set: 7:19/6:19
Day's Length: 11 hours
Average High/Low: 40/23
Average Temperature: 32
Record High: 69 – 1922, 71 – 2023
Record Low: - 10 – 1963

Weather

Today and tomorrow are typically the warmest days of the entire month. For the first time since December 12th there is a 25 percent chance of a high in the 60s, along with a 20 percent for one in the 50s. Forties occur 30 percent of the time, 30s twenty-five percent. Skies are cloudy 65 percent of the years in my record, with rain or snow likely 45 percent of the years.

Natural Calendar

The benign thaws of Early Spring tell mallards, canvasback ducks and killdeer to check out sites for laying eggs. Milder afternoons call out moths and water striders. Along highways, flocks of red-winged blackbirds and robins are out in the fields. In town, mourning cloak butterflies appear, and chipmunks come out to play and mate in the dwindling woodpiles. Ragwort, hemlock and dock grow back in the swamps.

Orion has moved off to the west these evenings. Regulus the central star of equinox, is halfway to its place in the middle of the sky, and Arcturus, which leads the Corona Borealis into June,

151

lies along the eastern horizon. By two in the morning, the Pleiades have set. Sirius is almost gone as well.

Daybook

1983: After a warm spell of several days, the first fly seen. Pussy willows half open.

1988: Rhubarb up, doves singing, high of 63 and wind to 50 miles an hour.

1990: First aconite flowers in the yard. Frances Hurie told me some of her aconites blossomed three weeks ago.

1992: First snowdrops bloomed today in 70-degree temperatures. One aconite came open in the middle of the afternoon. Pussy willows breaking out half way. First purple deadnettle flowered along the rose fence. Several flies out in the yard, two daffodils budding.

1995: Home from Jekyll Island. In the four days we were gone, half a dozen purple and pale yellow snow crocus and a new patch of snowdrops have budded.

1996: In the east garden, daffodil tips have emerged, snow crocus are getting taller, their foliage still yellow from having come up under the mulch. Early Spring weather has been here for three days now, and the ground is getting soft. First lamb's ears found.

1998: A large patch of golden snow crocus is in bloom today, and another patch of purples is about to come open. By the pond, the purple deadnettle is flowering, and even in the cooler east garden, the first two pale blue crocus have bloomed. Almost all the daffodils have buds now, and they could start opening any day. Peonies are up two to three inches, the highest I've ever recorded them at this date. First bleeding heart foliage heads seen. Crows seem louder these mornings. Geese flew over at 8:28 a.m. - first time this spring I've heard a flock near the house.

2000: Walking in the vegetable garden, I found a full-grown

opossum dead, lying across the brittle asparagus stalks.

2004: At 3:30 this morning, a skunk sprayed under the house. Very bad! Had to run the attic fan for hours to dilute the smell. But spring countered spring: cardinals sang at 6:50 this morning. By 7:30, the yard was full of the sounds of doves, crows, cardinals, grackles, squirrels. Henry Myers called this afternoon, minutes after he saw the first bluebirds on his property. A little later, I talked to Bob Barcus: "The buzzards were here all winter," he said. "They never left their roost on President Street."

2006: Field sparrow heard this morning when I was walking Bella. Robins all around.

2007: I heard a cardinal sing at 6:58 this morning.

2008: Cold continues, snow and sleet, the schools shut down again. At the feeders, starlings seem to be pushing out the giant flock of sparrows.

2009: Birmingham to Mobile and Dauphin Island. Blue jays courting, doves and cardinals calling at early morning in the campsite. The drive south was relatively uneventful, the road straight and lined with cutover scrub pine forest. Buzzards common, as they were yesterday. Cress noticed near Montgomery, had been in bloom for some time. Maples in bloom along the route, with a few buds greening as we moved further south. Since most of the land was in pines, the effect of the flowering trees was relatively light. One redbud, full blush, seen about 145 miles north of Mobile. Pelicans and egrets noticed as we reached the wetlands. Into Mobile: azaleas seen in full bloom, and one planting of multicolored tulips. Here at Dauphin Island, 845 miles from Yellow Springs, the air is in the 50s by the beach, the wind steady and chilly.

2010: On the last day of the first Early Spring thaw, Casey called to report 30 to 40 buzzards at their roost along Corey Street. He said he didn't know if they had spent the winter or had just returned but that they were "quite a flock."

2011: A villager called the police this week to say he had seen fifty eagles over town. The police responded and found two! More eagles than I've ever heard reported here.

2012: Crows at 7:05, cardinals singing throughout my walk at 9:00. Sun with high near 60 today, the snow crocus wide open in the south garden, honeybees among the flowers, their legs fat and orange with crocus pollen.

2013: From Fresno up the central valley of California: Crows scrawing in the dark well before daylight (much earlier than Ohio crows that always wait at least for twilight), small flocks out to scavenge while I packed the car and walked Bella under palm trees, the weather mild and the wind that had followed me from Ohio finally quiet. The sun came up with traffic along Highway 99 north, and I watched much of the same landscape of orchards and vineyards and green fields. Trucks of hay passed south of me, and haying (the first cut of the year) seems to have just been completed here.

The roadsides became richer the further north I drove, more gold and white cresses sometimes in drifts along the median, the roadside grasses getting lush and long. Orchards had only a few blossoms below Fresno, but were coming into full early bloom by Merced, maybe because of an increase of moisture. I found decorative pear trees full of flowers at a rest stop north of Sacramento. Still, only a few deciduous trees were getting leaves, and I saw a weeping willow that had not begun to turn yellow green – something that would have occurred in the Lower Midwest if pears were blooming. Towards Redding, a flurry of shrubs with pink and violet flowers, maybe weigelas, and some bushes with pale yellow flowers. Buzzards, absent since the desert, appeared in the sky again the further north I drove, crows no longer common, starling-like birds clustering on high wires and feeding by the side of the road.

The sun stayed out all day, even into the northern California mountains. I drove toward Mount Shasta, a massive white presence in the northern horizon, and I remembered childhood rides with my big sister in the rumble seat of an old Ford when our parents took us from Klamath Falls to the military base to see movies in 1944. Mount Shasta was always the main attraction.

And so I took a room with the view of Shasta while the sun was still out. But then in an hour or two, altostratus clouds moved across from the northwest, and then a lower great stratus bank settled down around the mountain and everything was gray.

2014: Bella and I went out to hear cardinals again this morning. They were five minutes earlier than three days ago: 6:48. The crows didn't pass over until 6:59. Geese were restless and calling at 7:10. Most significant of all: the first grackles of the year were at the feeder when I looked out the back door after breakfast. And John Blakelock called at 11:40 to tell me he had seen a flock of about forty or fifty sandhill cranes, just a few minutes previously, heading north pretty much right on schedule – and synchronized, it seems, with the arrival of the grackles. At the Covered Bridge in the afternoon, sky continued clear, 56 degrees: the river was still high, so fast and loud, gurgling, from the flooding of several days ago. The water had come in up to fifty feet in some places, and all the chickweed and grasses were dirtied and matted. The ragwort, however, was upright and bright, refreshed by flood and debris. Most of the skunk cabbage was still hidden in the swamp, but several plants were up about six inches, open and blooming.

2017: A fifth mild day, low in the 50s near sunrise: A small flock of grackles at the feeder again – and there was a robin chorus when I went outside a little after 7:00. So grackles may not only dovetail with sandhill cranes moving north, but with robins reaching critical mass. The koi were excited when I walked by the pond this morning; I went and got them some food, and they ate with moderate enthusiasm (but not the summer feasting). Ed Oxley reported lots of bees at his place today. Many leaves on the lower honeysuckle branches in the yard and Glen. First hepatica along the river, chickweed rising, first henbit flowering in the circle garden, first snow on the mountain in the dooryard, First forsythia buds ready to open along the street.

2018: Last week, another winter trip south from the deep northern thaw and Yellow Springs rains into the more pervasive thaw of the Gulf.

Intermittent botanizing, looking for seasonal landmarks: The landscape brown all the way through Louisville, Kentucky. Then near Bowling Green, March signs gathered: the greening of the fields and roadsides grew and grew. In the woods behind our motel in Athens, Alabama, just above the Tennessee border, we could hear tree frogs, shrill and steady above the rumble of trucks.

One early forsythia bush, some white clover and one dandelion at a rest stop halfway to Birmingham, and then fifty miles later, Middle Spring emerged with daffodils and plum blossoms, and then after Montgomery into northern Florida: pink magnolias, red quince and full redbuds.

Such sparse markers open other channels, compressing time and events, parts standing for the whole, only suggesting what happens in the temporal and geographic gaps that occur in rapid travel.

When I walked a portion of the Camino de Santiago in northwestern Spain in March and April last year, I moved so slowly that I could almost follow spring as it developed. By driving to the Gulf in two days this past week, I traveled only to destinations, skipped across hundreds of miles of floral time, lost the meat of the seasons, arrived at April without March.

Carrying the awareness of local walks from previous years with me to connect the dots, however, I could play with memories and associations. The redbuds and the pink magnolias and the tree frogs evoked not only dates and experiences from my notebooks but also elusive psychic spaces. Personal natural history was a cue for fantasy.

All of the material world and its transformations and its connections were evocative forms, flimsy and web-like, fog-like, mists of images and feelings that created a true phenology of parallels within which not only did the part represent the whole, but also the signs, conjuring emotion and knowledge, became what they signified.

2019: Frost, 30 degrees, light breeze: Crows at 6:50 this morning, cardinals just a few second later – and then steady throughout my walk. Doves at exactly 7:00 a.m. No robin chorus yet. Casey called with a positive ID of a red-winged blackbird. As I worked outside cutting off bamboo that had been killed by the below-zero days, a tufted titmouse sang steadily from the hackberry tree.

2020: Driving along Clifton Road this afternoon, Jill an I came upon a behemoth flock of grackles swarming in a cut-over cornfield.

2021: The morning mild, wind moaning in the trees, snow melting, thaw. And Mary Sue writes: "We had a group of red-winged blackbirds early this morning, February 22, earlier than last year when they appeared on Leap Day, February 29." And Jeff, visiting his daughter-in-law for her birthday, heard sandhill cranes calling overhead in the county.

2022: Hard rain and winds all day, second afternoon in the 60s, major flooding from here into northern Indiana. The backyard is soggy and full of puddles. And Chris writes from 35 miles north: "All of a sudden, birds are back. The first red-winged blackbird arrived last Thursday (the 17th). Now there are many. So good to hear their songs again. Red-tailed hawks are very active now. And tonight—woodcocks! First ones of the season, and multiple ones! We heard one singing its peent song, while at the same time we could hear two more doing their aerial ballet somewhere in the dusk. Also, heard the first spring peeper Sunday evening (the 20th)."

And Jack called from Winter Street, paying respects to the late Ed Oxley (always the first to have snowdrops in bloom), and reporting snowdrops flowering overnight, daffodils suddenly up, hellebores budded, crocus emerged and budded overnight. "They know when it's time!" he said. Later, Casey left a message: first glimpse of red-wings in his yard.

2023: A gradual warming through the day to reach a new record high of 71 degrees. The second daffodil opened. Sedum foliage has emerged and the deep-purple standard crocuses have opened by the back porch. In the dooryard, quince buds show a little green. A few hundred miles to the north, a blizzard sweeps across Minneapolis, Madison, Chicago and moves east.

Journal

It is Early Spring, and I collect the pieces of the changes, watching them accumulate and spread. There are not enough pieces yet to make a full-fledged spring, but I know that they will come if I recall them. And so I build a scaffolding on which to place them when I find them, a skeleton on which to fashion the new season.

All of natural history is in my favor on the 22nd of February. If I compress my Yellow Springs notes from that day, going back to 1983, I can fabricate a quilt of events, webs of color and sound and warming winds to weave into the frame of a twenty-four hour span.

Then, a circadian shape appears, a four-dimensional psychic set, the radius of casual observation cutting across my eighty years, cross-sectioning time (albeit with bias against winter) and I fill in the empty spaces of my imaginary structure of backyard natural history, requiring only this one day to make spring arrive.

I encounter the first fly on this date in 1983, pussy willows half open then. Rhubarb is up in 1988 to the singing of doves and the heat of 63 degrees. Bright yellow aconites are in bloom in 1990. Snowdrops are flowering in 1992, and under a high of 70, there are flies in the yard and two daffodils budding and violet lamium blossoming.

I arrive back from Georgia in 1995 to find half a dozen purple and pale yellow snow crocuses. This day in 1996, the daffodils are starting to unravel. Slick, red peony stalks are up three inches in 1998, and the soft leaves of the bleeding heart are pushing out.

The early morning of 2004 is filled with the sounds of doves, crows, cardinals, sparrows, starlings (singing before seven o'clock), and Henry calls to report a bluebird. Then I am surrounded by robins along the river in 2006. Casey reports three-dozen buzzards at their roost on Corry Street. There are honeybees among the new crocuses in 2012, their legs fat and orange with pollen. On the 22nd in 2014, the first flock of grackles arrives in the back yard, about the same time that John reports sandhill cranes on their way north. The robin chorus begins this day in

2017, the earliest I've ever heard it. On February 22, 2021, Mary Sue announced the arrival red-winged blackbirds at Ellis Pond. And Jeff heard sandhill cranes.

All of Early Spring is right here in one day. And there is nothing false about such a composite. Its selectivity, ignoring the cold and snowy 22nds, is less self-deception than prophesy. Precedent is the cloak that dresses the bare frame of February. It tells me where and when I was and am and soon will be.

Although a life of retreat offers various joys, none, I think, will compare with the time one employs in the study of herbs, or in striving to gain some practical knowledge of nature's domain.

Walafrid-Strabo, *Hortulus*, 9th Century A.D.

February 23rd
The 54th Day of the Year

We felt the stir of hall and street,
The pulse of life that round us beat;
The chill embargo of the snow
Was melted in the genial glow;
Wide swung again our ice-locked door,
And all the world was ours once more.

John Greenleaf Whittier

Sunrise/set: 7:18/6:20
Day's Length: 11 hours 2 minutes
Average High/Low: 40/23
Average Temperature: 32
Record High: 68 – 1985, 70 – 2017 and 2023
Record Low: - 7 – 1885

Weather

Chances of a day in the 50s or 60s are 15 to 20 percent each, with 40s occurring 40 percent of the afternoons. There is just a 15 percent chance of 20s and a ten percent chance of 30s. As the 21st century progresses, the possibility of 70s becomes more and more likely. The sun shines twice as often today as yesterday, and that phenomenon marks the beginning of the end of winter's gray skies. Although February and March still have plenty of clouds in store, the frequency of brighter days now shows a slow but steady advance.

Natural Calendar

Migrant crows return with their young, sometimes clashing with the crows that have spent the winter in the North. In Lake Erie, the steelhead salmon run, which started in the fall, comes to a close. After Snowdrop Winter (often between February 23rd and 27th), ducks and geese follow the lead of the blackbirds, marking ownership of the more favorable river sites for nesting. More migrant robins join the sizeable flocks that overwintered in the exurban woodlands, and when enough robins have gathered, the numbers give rise to their pre-dawn mating chorus.

Daybook

1984: Rhubarb is up. Jane Morgan's snowdrops are blooming.
A moth was fluttering at the greenhouse window about 9:00 p.m.

1985: Bill Mullins said he saw a robin on his lawn yesterday.
Grape hyacinths are up north of the forsythia. One peony stalk
seen. Tulips, daffodils and rhubarb are pushing out a little. Crows
restless, loud in the mornings.

1986: Mock orange buds are turning green.

1987: Cardinal sings at 6:50 a.m. Clear skies.

1988: Doves singing by 7:20 a.m. They continue through the day.
An inch of snow on the ground after yesterday's high of 63. Pussy
willows a third out.

1991: Tulips up one to three inches throughout the yard. First
snowdrops open. One crocus budding. Even with the temperature
remaining below 40 degrees, the sun is strong. We're all restless.
Neysa just left to wander downtown. Jeanie felt lost. I am
struggling to do winter chores. My instinct is to be off to the woods
and the water.

1992: First golden crocus blooms. Cardinal seen with straw in its
beak.

1995: Roadkills have increased significantly this week: opossums
and skunks. First purple deadnettle flowers in the garden today,
and the very first yellow snow crocus.

2000: The first crocus of the year opened today in the east garden,
four purple ones by 9:30 a.m. In the south garden by the pond, the
first two golds were open by 11:00. And as I walked up to check
the pond, something darted away in the water, maybe the first frog
or toad of the millennium. North of town into the countryside this
afternoon: no maples blooming. Some locust pods on the path, had

probably fallen in the past week or so.

2001: Suzi's aconites are open in the snow. At home, tulip foliage is up two inches.

2002: First cardinal at 6:46 this morning. Sky clear, frost and 18 degrees. In the yard, pussy willows have emerged about a fourth of the way.

2004: Jeanie reports that Bryan reports that Janet Hackett's snowdrops are blooming. (Bryan bought Janet's house after she died.) Our snowdrops are budded, one of them almost ready to open.

2005: The animal-trapping man from Enon came by to check the traps here at the house. He said that he had been getting a lot of calls about skunks and had been catching a lot of raccoons, but he didn't catch our critter.

2008: In spite of continued cold and snow, cardinals were singing near 7:00 this morning. Coming from Beavercreek on the backroad tonight, Jeanie and I drove through a potent cloud of skunk odor!

2009: Dauphin Island, Alabama: Walked the bird sanctuary under sunny skies, a cool wind from the Gulf, high in the middle 50s. Found one blue spiderwort in bloom, sprawling brambles of white-flowered wild blackberries, patches of black medic clover, scattered yellow wood sorrel, violet bearded flowers on a thin-leafed rosemary-like plant (a sandhill rosemary or beach heather), a yellow-orange blooming woody plant, all in a habitat of live oaks, sand live oaks, yaupon (with bark like crepe myrtles), magnolias (with thin flower buds), wandering greenbrier, sawtooth palmetto, basal leaves of thistles, wild lettuce a foot high, pokeweed two feet high, withered bracken – its new growth not yet emerging, pennywort with buds (in the Magnolia Park). Pelicans and gulls and other sea birds seen out in the water. A foot-long shark had washed up on shore.

2010: At 7:30 this morning, I heard the first dove of the year calling. In the greenhouse, small ants were crawling all over the table where I was working. And the snow melted enough to show clumps of snowdrops sticking up, their white tips strong, obvious.

2011: Crows at 7:00. Light snow on the ground, cloudy and 29 degrees in the late morning, cardinals singing throughout my walk in the neighborhood.

2012: Geese and cardinals at 6:55, and the first grackles of the year arrived at the feeder before 8:00 and calling throughout the morning. Aconites hold at early bloom in the alley, a few henbits open there now, and, in the north garden, the first bittercress flowers opening. From Dandridge, Tennessee, Jeff and Kit report finding the first daffodils of their trip south. Tonight when we went to be, a rumble of thunder (the first of the year) south over Xenia.

2013: Northern California to Portland, Oregon: The forecast was for another winter storm overnight, but there was very little accumulation at the motel. Mount Shasta was still covered in white stratus clouds when I took off, accompanied by the crows. The highway was clear for a while, but then the pass into Oregon was icy, and visibility was reduced to almost nothing when I reached 4,000 feet. After I dropped down below the clouds into the valley, flurries became steady rain, the roadside grasses turned long and green, fields were lush. Golden cress bloomed again, and I saw open yellow crocus, and bittercress. A small white-flowered aster-like flower blossomed in the grass of rest stops. Daffodils were budding, just about like I left them in the circle garden at home.

Arriving in Portland, I received a message from Mike in Yellow Springs: "Today must have been 'robin day' on the south end of town. There were robins all over the Dollar General, YSI and Springs Motel area. Also, I made a batch of the best maple syrup I ever tasted yesterday. Yield from approximately five gallons was one pint."

2014: I talked to Bob Barcus and to Casey today, and they both said they had heard the yodel of a red-winged blackbird – which makes sense, since the redwings usually arrive at the same time as the grackles. And at 4:00 p.m., Audrey Hackett contacted me to say she and her husband had seen a flock of sandhills over their house at Pleasant Street and Park Place. But she said they were flying southwest.

2016: The weather is sunny and mild in the 50s, violet snow crocus and snowdrops in full flower here and about town. Algae building up in the pond, and I began water treatments today. The first white standard crocus bloomed in the south garden by noon.

2017: A sixth mild day in the 60s. Robins were in chorus when I went outside at 6:38 this morning, most likely had been singing since at least 6:30. At Ed Oxley's land by the Miami River: large patches of snowdrops, the small and large varieties, one clump of deep-purple iris reticulata, large aging aconites, many snow crocus and some standard crocuses, stonecrop foliage about three inches (like at the post office). At home, many forsythia flowers fully open, one daffodil slowly unraveling, some standard crocuses, white and purple. Peony, daffodil and hyacinth stalks surging, a few more squills showing, the first bittercress. Lilac buds fat and green, starting to come undone. Boxwood, red quince and Japanese honeysuckle leafing. Later in the day, Ed called to say he had seen a garter snake out in the sun.

2018: Jekyll Island, Georgia to Hillsville, Virginia (just above the border with North Carolina): I was surprised to see the vegetation markers quite consistent all the way from south of Savanna to about Statesville, North Carolina: Jessamine climbing in the woods and fences – more than I've ever seen, daffodils, plums, white clover, pears, red maples and several other tree varieties in bloom. Live oaks with fresh leaves. It seems that damage from the severe freezes of a month ago has been negated by the recent warmth and moisture.

2019: I slept too late to hear the first cardinals, but when I went out with Ranger at 7:30, I walked into a small flock of robins peeping and whinnying at the corner of High and Dayton. A couple hours later, Emily wrote to say she had heard robins around 10:00 a.m. At Ellis, there still are hundreds of geese, but they are restless, some in the soybean fields, some in pasture, dozens flying back and forth. In one field at the north end of the pond, I saw robins. Numerous snowdrops with their white buds turned down but stil not open. From Springfield, Leah reports seeing a snowy owl by the side of the road, "just like he was one of those road hawks."

2020: Leah reports red-winged blackbirds at her feeders north of town.

2021: Another news story today about how 2020 and 2016 were the warmest years ever recorded for the planet. But a stabilizing note from Michele at Flying Mouse Farm: "Well, as you know, the cold weather stopped the sap in its tracks right after we tapped. So I'm writing to let you know the sap started flowering yesterday and there is plenty to collect today. Now I suppose the season has started!" In the fields beyond Ellis Pond this afternoon, the geese were conversing long and loud, not hunkered down like they have been. And a high in the upper 40s today. Song sparrows heard at the Glass Farm wetland.

2022: When Bill Mullins saw a robin on this day in 1985, I took it to be the "first robin" of spring. In fact, it was one of the parts of the major robin migration that moves through this area at the end of (or perhaps throughout) February.

2023: Another near-record day. Birds strong this morning at 7:00, but no robin singsong. Casey in midmorning: four red-winged blackbirds, the first, at his feeder, George Bieri at 11:30 reporting sandhill cranes, about a dozen. "I don't know what that bodes," he commented, "but I just wanted to let you know." Then I went looking for snow trillium at the mill habitat in the afternoon warmth. The river was high from the rains of the past week, the land brown with leaves, chickweed spreading, one bittercress flower seen, some feathery harbinger-of-spring foliage peeking out, many low honeysuckle branches leafing, no snow trilliums. But at the post office in town, a great patch of Baby Blue Eyes (*veronica*) in full bloom. In Jill's back entryway, a few dozen Asian ladybeetles were crawling about. And to the quarry before sundown: red-winged blackbirds were boisterous setting territories. Distant calls of what seemed like killdeers. So far in the month, the average temperature is 40.0, about eight degrees above normal.

All nature is but art, unknown to thee;
All chance, direction which thou canst not see.

Alexander Pope

In understanding based on direct experience, however, there is no right or wrong, no good or evil. When spring comes, spring comes; when winter is gone, winter is gone.

Katsuki Sekida

Sunrise/set: 7:16/6:21
Day's Length: 11 hours 5 minutes
Average High/Low: 41/23
Average Temperature: 32
Record High: 67 – 1930, 76 – 2017
Record Low: - 3 – 1914

Weather

This is typically one of the windiest times of February (the sixth high pressure system often arrives within 24 hours of today), and colder temperatures often return for Snowdrop Winter. While 50s and 60s each come five percent of the time, and 40s are recorded 40 percent of the years, highs only in the 30s occur 30 percent of the time, 20s fifteen percent and teens five percent. Snow falls 35 percent of the years. Rain falls another 15 percent, and skies are completely overcast more than half the time.

Natural Calendar

If pastures are ready, livestock is wormed before being turned out to pasture when February draws to a close. Mares show signs of estrus as the days grow longer. The last of the lambs and kids conceived in middle autumn are born. Chipmunks come out to play and mate in the sun. Rabbits are breeding; foxes will be hunting them.

Daybook

1984: Covered Bridge: Buckeye buds are swelling. Raspberry leaves have started; one seems fully developed. Clover is growing. Wild onions have put on an inch or two. New ragwort and leafcup foliage near the spring. More aster leaves and fresh dandelions along the paths. One touch-me-not has sprouted. A small white moth flew past me towards the river.

1985: Lily-of-the-valley up half an inch in front of the house. Pussy willows begin to emerge after seven thaw days. First bee of the year seen in 67-degree weather.

1987: Cardinal at 6:44 a.m. First fly of the year in my office.

1989: Close to zero this morning, but the cardinals are very loud, males defending territories.

1990: Tremendous storm blew all day. Temperatures dropped from the 30s into the teens. Two inches of snow. The barometer rose from 950 to 985 in 24 hours. Wind to 45 mph. River high and fast. But the first robin came to High Street at 3:25 p.m.

1993: High pressure moves in today, after days of flurries. Close to zero at 6:00 a.m. Jeni called at noon: the azaleas in Jacksonville are almost in full bloom. They really started opening a week ago, she said.

1994: From Jacksonville, Jeni says everything is yellow with pollen today.

1996: As the weather warms, white clover and purple deadnettle are among the most precocious plants to extend new leaves.

2000: Snowdrop winter didn't come this year. The temperature reached closed to 70 today in Yellow Springs, came within a degree short of the record at the airport. Eleven purple crocus opened in the east garden, four snowdrops. Pansies have arrived at the nurseries. Pussy willows are pushing out all at once. To Springfield and back: no crows seen flying, just one small flock in the woods near school. Probably the biggest motion of spring today was the waking of the two koi, Emmet and Zelda in the pond. When I saw them swimming, I checked the water temperature: 50 degrees.

2004: On the way to Washington Court House this morning, I noticed that the farm ponds had begun to show some open water; they've been frozen over since early January. This afternoon, Anita Swetland called, said she was awakened at 9:00 by two Carolina wrens beating against her window, trying to get out of her bedroom. "They'd come in through the window I'd left open for the cat!" she explained. "I guess they were looking for a place to make a nest." The wrens eventually made it outside the way they came, and Anita was cheered by their visit: "Spring is just around the corner!" she told me several times in the course of our conversation. At home, the skunk is still under the house: another strong spray at 11:30 p.m.

2006: In South Glen, the wingstem seed heads have contracted as the seeds disappeared through the winter. Ironweed heads are tight and fragile. Yellow fruit of the horse nettle still holds in the fields, shriveled but bright against the pale grass. A few rose hips are hanging on, but they fell easily if I touched them. Euonymus and bittersweet berries still intact on the ground.

2007: A cardinal was singing at 6:55 this morning. Henry Myers called this afternoon to report seeing a buzzard flying over Stevenson Road at about noon. The highs have been in the 30s this week, and sleet is forecast for tonight.

2008: Cardinals were singing at 6:49 this morning, the day very cold, the sky clear. When I walked Bella in the alley around 10:00, a male cardinal was courting two females in the honeysuckle bushes, and other males were singing all around me.

2009: Dauphin Island to north of Baton Rouge, Morganza, Louisiana: White clover, tall ragwort, sow thistles common along the roadside, trees budding – many maples with large red seed clusters. New cattails were at least waist high. Full redbud seen above Baton Rouge, and then at the Rosedown Plantation, we found camellias in full bloom, full rhododendrons, tulips, daffodils, late azaleas. By the roads, tall ragwort, a few giant white thistles, blooming dock, wild onions setting fruit, and egrets in the wetlands. One yellow sulphur butterfly seen along the freeway, the only butterfly so far this trip. Temperature in the 60s and partly cloudy skies, low only going into the 50s tonight.

2011: Another brief thaw, and more snowdrops have emerged from their sheaths, many snow crocus leaves are fully developed, the later crocus up almost an inch, and daffodils up to three inches, all of this taking place in the cold and snow of the past week. Walking down the alley this morning, I heard cardinals all the way.

2012: Mild this morning, but hard gusts of wind, flurries predicted for tonight. In the alley, more aconites are in full bloom, even though the temperature has not gone much above 50. In front of the Village Artisans store, a few mouse-eared chickweed buds are opening.

2013: Portland, Oregon: At Jeni's house, fat, purple mid-season crocuses are coming in. This morning when I went out to walk Bella at 6:40, a cardinal and my crows were calling, maybe just a little earlier than they do in Yellow Springs on this date. But after 3,300 miles, I have come through March and April to the February from where I began when I left Ohio.

2014: Walking Bella before sunrise, light wind, perfectly clear, Venus big in the southeast, the fourth-quarter moon leading her on: Doves at 6:45, one cardinal at 6:46, the other cardinals waiting until 6:50, song sparrow at 6:56.

2016: Heavy rain through the night, windy, mild and overcast when I woke up around 5:30. Then at 5:37, a cardinal sang several times – an hour early – and then was quiet. Perhaps it was the full moon, hidden by heavy stratus clouds but still brightening the sky a little, that fooled him. Snow forecast for tomorrow.

2017: The seventh and last day of this February heat wave. The daffodils opened all the way overnight, and two more opened throughout the day. March 6 (in 1983, 1992, 2000) was the earliest date recorded to this point in the year. Grackles now grackle with the robins after sunrise. Robins seen mating outside the studio windows. The first white cabbage butterfly came to the dooryard garden as I came out onto the front porch. More mosquitoes, more crocus, more budding daffodils. In South Glen, multiflora roses leafing, small ichneumons fluttering ahead of us. Spring peepers reported by Chris north of town,

2018: Hillsville, Virginia, to Yellow Springs in heavy rain: Trees blooming and even a willow pale green through the mountains, flowering disappearing and the landscape becoming mostly brown when we reached Ohio. At home, the bamboo has been shedding, the pond netting covered with its leaves. the snowdrops in the yard were all in full flower, and the Lenten roses had opened. Some crocus were budded, may have opened in the warmer days of last week. In the soggy ground of the circle garden, the daffodils were up about eight inches and a few had buds. Squills were up. Clusters of basal stonecrop foliage have appeared. The lungwort has a few leaves now. Red tips of peonies show through the leaves. Poppies are growing back. The first tulips are an inch tall.

2019: After a high this morning in the 50s (the barometer down to 29.40), a wind storm came east, blowing hard throughout the the day, barometer remaining at 29.40. In spite of the wind, I heard the first cardinal at 6:45, a few robin peeps, and then the steady call of a tufted titmouse. In the middle of the storm, Chris heard the "peent" of a woodcock. Jill drove home today from Rochester, NY, in gusts up to 50 mph.

2020: Casey called: He saw the first red-winged blackbird of the year at his feeder; it was chasing away the grackles.

2021: The thaw quickens: 59 degrees with a southwest wind today, snow melting inch by inch. The white tips of snowdrops peer through the newly liberated tangle of euonymus vines in the dooryard. Three daffodil spears about three inches high noticed as the snow melted on the other side of the walk. Casey reports red-winged blackbirds at his feeders now, mostly immature males, he says.

2022: A winter storm approaches to punctuate Snowdrop Winter. Across the Atlantic, Russia invades Ukraine, putting an end to the

European peace of the past thirty years and placing issues about global warming, sea-level rise and species extinction in the perspective of possible nuclear holocaust, the final great extinction in human history. It makes me feel like I am journaling at the end of the world.

Journal

I started my counting practice decades ago when I was trying to stop smoking. Counting cigarettes was entryway, a threshold to control. The fewer cigarettes I counted, the more self-control I had. Even if I counted too many, at least I had counted. I had not failed so much as I had tried and succeeded at trying.

These days, tobacco long ago controlled for now, I still count. Several years ago, I started to count the number of my lily plants that came into bloom. Soon, that was not enough. I had to count the number of actual blossoms that were open.

And then two years ago, I put in dozens and dozens of daffodil and tulip bulbs, and then I started counting them when they flowered last spring. There were just the right amount of flowers to count. And now this year, the first daffodils in my yard bloomed on February 21, and then with way-above average temperatures, I had two daffodils on the 22nd and three on the 24th. So the great counting begins again.

With the cigarettes, I was practicing self-control. One obsession replaced another. With the daffodils, I was and am actually giving in to just counting, just having an excuse for counting. I am practicing self-indulgence instead of self-mastery. It's an escape from non-counting, from having to make sense.

Counting one thing is always about counting something else. Totals mean less than repetition. Practice is more important than outcomes. Intent changes the equation, makes its own value, transforms context, skews the math to its own designs. This morning, more daffodils are coming in, That's all that matters.

February 25th
The 56th Day of the Year

As yet the trembling year is unconfirm'd,
And Winter oft at eve resumes the breeze,
Chills the pale morn, and bids his driving sleets
Deform the day delightless.

James Thomson

Sunrise/set: 7:15/6:22
Day's Length: 11 hours 7 minutes
Average High/Low: 41/24
Average Temperature: 32
Record High: 69 – 1930
Record Low: - 9 – 1900

Weather

During the second day of Snowdrop Winter, highs in the 50s or 60s are rarely recorded. Highs in the 40s occur almost 30 percent of the time, 30s forty percent, 20s twenty-five percent, and chances of a high only in the teens are five percent for the last time this season. Snow falls on almost half of the years in my weather history, making the 25th the day most likely to bring frozen precipitation in the entire second month.

Natural Calendar

Every landscape is, as it were, a state of the soul, and whoever penetrates into both is astonished to find how much likeness there is in each detail.

Henri Frederic Amiel

y

The very earliest bulbs, the snowdrops the snow crocus and the aconites, have already bloomed in the sunniest microclimates. Now it is time for the larger, brighter standard crocus and the small spring iris, the *iris reticulate,* to flower in warmer springs..

When one thing happens, something else is always

happening, too. The flowering of those bulbs bears witness to the blossoming of silver maples and the red maples along city streets, the blooming of weedy henbit in the garden, the increasing flow of maple sap, the full emergence of pussy willows, the appearance of woolly bear caterpillars, the full bloom of the snow trillium along the rivers, the full bloom of skunk cabbage, the time for woodcocks to arrive from the South and for juncos to depart for the North.

Daybook

1984: Purple crocus buds seen on Walnut Street, new catnip leaves growing nearby. First grape hyacinth foliage is up in the lawn at home. Motherwort leaves strong by the woodshed.

1985: One daffodil in front of the bookstore downtown has a bud.

1986: Marc Heeg calls: two robins seen near downtown.

1987: First robin seen at Wilberforce today. First daffodil with a bud in front of the bookstore. Cardinal sings at 6:45 a.m.

1988: Cardinal sang at 6:52 a.m. One leaf of rhubarb emerged from the mulch today.

1989: First groundhog of the year seen feeding by the side of Grinnell Road.

1990: Pussy willows, almost completely emerged, complement the snow blown onto the branches by yesterday's storm.

1991: Squirrel runs in front of the car, almost hit. First time I've come across a squirrel so disoriented since autumn.

1995: Jeni calls from Portland, Oregon. Daffodils in bloom everywhere, trees flowering. It's spring in the Northwest, she says.

1996: A week ago all the grass was brown. Now it's getting a touch of green.

1998: First red-winged blackbird of the year seen this morning along Dayton-Yellow Springs Road. On Limestone Street, five forsythia flowers have opened. *Cornus mas* on Corey Street is blooming. First honeysuckle leaves unraveling in South Glen.

2000: More wonderful warmth, and the crocus are coming out all at once, twenty in the south garden, over thirty in the east garden. Scattered dandelions blooming. A spotted frog came out to sun on the rocks by the side of the pond. I heard a red-winged blackbird calling on the way to Fairborn. At the Cascades, most foliage is still not visible, but at one spot near the water, there were buds on a tight cluster of violet cress. Catalpa beans hold. The great flock of winter crows seems to have left Springfield.

2001: Full snow crocus patch in the south garden. Pussy willows maybe a third out. Maple full bloom at the park.

2004: First cardinal song at 6:44 this morning. Bryan reports that Janet Hackett's snowdrops are blooming.

2005: Greg called this morning at about 11:40. "Have you been watching the blackbirds?" he asked. I went outside, and thousands of blackbirds were crossing the village from north to south. They had been flying over for about half an hour, Greg said. This afternoon, Bob Barcus stopped me in front of the credit union; he asked if I'd seen any signs of spring. Of course, he added, buzzards were no news – they'd spent the winter here for the second or third year in a row.

2006: Full bloom of snowdrops, aconites and snow crocus. Maple sap running strong in the sun, and temperatures in the 50s.

2009: Morganza, Louisiana to Columbus, Texas: Roadside fleabane, sow thistles and tall ragwort, some red maples with large leaf-like seed clusters. We drive across the scrub bayou land of western Louisiana into the dry windy flats of eastern Texas. High in the 70s today, but the landscape is still brown and winter-like. All along the Gulf coast, some budding and small leafing taking place on deciduous trees, but those trees are such a minority among the cut-over pines that the impression remains one of Late Winter. From Columbus, Ohio, Frank Doden wrote: "Just thought you'd like to know. I saw a honeybee at 12:10 p.m.

2010: Greg Schaur called to report he had seen a herring gull in Centerville, a rare winter resident. They usually migrate in late fall and Early Spring.

2011: In the middle of a snowstorm, I heard cardinals a little before 7:00 this morning.

2012: The red tips of peonies have finally started coming up, well behind the full blooming snowdrops, hellebores, aconites and snow crocus.

2013: "Signs of spring!" said Rebecca's five-year-old daughter, Merida. "We saw a bunch of birds flying around us when we were on our way to Home Depot." And: "On the golf course when I was at school, there was the first little dandelion!" Ed Oxley called a little later, citing honeybees on the 24th, buzzards on the outskirts of town, even one over King's Yard. And lots of robins and two ospreys along the river.

2016: Steep barometric rise today from yesterday's 29.25 (the lowest I remember it being), gusty wind and light snow.

2017: Strong wind, thunder and rain last night, cold front moving in hard with flurries now, snowdrop winter. In spite of the storm, the clump of daffodils is still standing straight this morning. At 6:25 this morning, I could hear sporadic robin peeps. Ten minute later, definite conversations. The north end of South Stafford Street was covered with maple flowers and hulls. Fourteen days above 50 so far this month, nine above 60, two above 70.

2019: The barometer, which began yesterday at 29.40 was up to 30.35 this morning. At 6:30, the wind still hard and cold, the gibbous moon almost overhead, Jupiter trailing behind, Venus following Jupiter so that the procession crossed half the sky. I thought I heard one cardinal at 6:40. Finally, the windstorm that had lasted over 24 hours (the longest I ever remember here) abated around 8:00 a.m. The day is bright and crisp, snowdrops well budded in the dooryard, pussy willows white against the robin's-egg-blue sky, and Leslie and Bruce wrote that they found three aconites flowering on their property. Then as Jill and I walked to the library in the late afternoon, we saw a great planting of aconites all blooming near the front of a house on Davis Street.

2023: Three daffodils in bloom today, half a dozen more waiting. Aida writes: " Was bicycling home yesterday around 3:00 p.m., north on the bike path from Xenia, and just before the heron rookery and and the ammunition factory I heard spring peepers. What a delight."

Journal
All that I had dreamed was true, is true.
The earth is fair, more fair
Than I had known or imagined.

Harlan Hubbard

In the Early Spring of the Ohio Valley, islands of new life emerge from the waves of warmth and cold that move across the landscape. Within these islands, often separated from each other by broad expanses of chilling winds, weeks of gray skies, sometimes only narrowly divided by a night of frost, the season reveals its stunning topography.

Early Spring is an archipelago of forms rising out of February's great sea, and like ephemeral atolls, the events of this temporal, mottled continent multiply, swell, and recede to alter the face of our habitat with an inexorable beauty. The geography of Early Spring is fixed in shape and order but not in time. The archipelago of winter's end is fluid, what chronologists call a "floating sequence," a sequence the dates of which are relatively well known in relation to one another but not in relation to when exactly they will occur on the brittle Gregorian calendar.

Observation and memory, however, easily decipher the secret code of the floating sequence, uncover the fluid terrain from which fauna and flora materialize, and spread a map of promise across the seemingly uncharted expanse of winter. In Yellow Springs, Early Spring fills the six weeks between the middle of February and the end March. This month and a half links the deep cold with the lushness of April, and it is made up of constellations of color, motion and sound, and musterings of new sprouts and leaves, birds, insects, mammals and fishes. In the South, this season can arrive in the middle of the year's first weeks; along the Canadian border, it comes in May. Wherever the floating sequence begins, it follows something of the order below; no matter where it takes place, the following landmarks are only fragments of a far greater ferment.

Starting with the major thaw of February's third week, the first cluster of spring's appearance takes the form of snowdrops and aconites flowering together in the warmest microclimates beside the prophetic hellebores and Chinese witchhazels of late January. Within a few days, snow crocus and *iris reticulata* complete this island of time at the chilliest edge of spring.

A parallel cluster rises from the swamps: the skunk cabbage blossoms at Jacoby. In alleyways and lawns, common chickweed, dandelions and henbit complement the cabbage. Above them all, red-winged blackbirds stake out different limits.

After Snowdrop Winter (between February 23rd and 27th), ducks and geese follow the lead of the blackbirds, marking ownership of the more favorable river sites for nesting. Migrant robins join the sizeable flocks that overwintered in the Glen.

Past the seasons of the snowdrops and aconites, midseason crocuses initiate more complex configurations that lead to fat pussy willows, bright blue squills, delicate yellow jonquils, then to the full-size daffodils, then to purple grape hyacinths, then to pale wood hyacinths and pushkinias. Towering on the horizon, silver maples and the red maples and box elders prepare to fruit.

To these outcroppings come the pollen seekers: the honeybees and carpenter bees. Other creatures follow. Mosquitoes and newborn wolf spiders look for prey. The mounds of ants rise from winter's prairie. In rivers and ponds, water striders mate. Earthworms come out of hiding, lie together in the mild night rains. It is salamander season in the slime and snake basking season in the sun. Spring peepers peep.

Then the root and insect eaters become active, joining the beavers that have been cutting trees and eating bark since January. Groundhogs dig up the hillsides. Opossums, skunks, raccoons come seek their mates and sustenance. Turkey vultures circle the roads looking for road kill. Wild turkeys start to call. The first woodcocks spiral in the woods. In the village, the tufted titmouse spirals, too.

When pussy willows are at their peak, new configurations take shape, adding multiple pathways to all the recent temporal spaces. Into the world of pussy willows come the white magnolias in town, snow trillium along the Little Miami, spring beauties on the college green. Across the bottomland, soft touch-me-nots sprout, coveted ramps push up their medicinal foliage to pace the stalks of daylilies, rhubarb and precocious bleeding hearts.

When pollen covers the pussy willows, then honeysuckle, mock orange, privet, wild multiflora roses, lilac, black raspberry and coralberry leaves break out from their buds, a signal for *Cornus mas* and lungwort to flower and for mourning cloak butterflies and cabbage moths to navigate the channels of equinox. A few days later come the question-mark and tortoise-shell butterflies and then the white-spotted skippers.

In the last few days of March when the pussy willow catkins start to fall, the archipelago of Early Spring becomes a dense maze of islets unimaginable at the end of February. In the trees, the finches turn gold. In ponds, the toads are singing. Calves and lambs appear in the fields. Carp are frolicking in the rivers. Young opossums come out to play. Wasps crawl from their winter crevices.

In the garden, the early tulips unfold. Star of Holland comes in beneath the bright forsythia. Buckeyes unravel along Grinnell Road. Plums bloom on Xenia Avenue. And just as skunk cabbage starts to produce its foliage at Jacoby, the first tremendous mass of wildflowers suddenly opens all at once on the farthest and mildest border of the Early Spring archipelago: inflorescence of periwinkle, hepatica, violet cress, harbinger of spring, bloodroot, Dutchman's britches, bittercress, twinleaf and Virginia bluebell leading now into the endlessly intricate paradise of April

February 26th
The 57th Day of the Year

Over prairie,
Over the prairie and the hills,
Crows fly, the winter spills
Down February's end.

August Derleth

Sunrise/set: 7:13/6:23
Day's Length: 11 hours 10 minutes
Average High/Low: 41/24
Average Temperature: 33
Record High: 69 – 1944
Record Low: - 8 – 1963

Weather

Today usually brings continued cold: highs in the 60s are rare; 50s come up to five percent of the time; 40s occur just 25 percent of the years, 30s forty-five percent, and 20s a full 25 percent. Below-zero mornings, however, are unusual. Skies are clear 65 percent of the time, and the likelihood of precipitation drops to only 25 percent.

Natural Calendar

"*I wanted to be a part of this awakening, not a mere beholder who only half understood what was going on.*

Charles Burchfield, *Journal,* February 25, 1912

When the early bulbs come in, clover grows back in the pastures and the tops of nettles in the sun are big enough for supper greens; celandine and garlic mustard and sweet rocket grow bushy in the alleys; violet leaves and horseradish leaves sprout in the garden. Honeysuckle leaves unravel on the branches closest to the ground. Buds lengthen and brighten on multiflora roses, mock orange, and lilac. Bleeding heart foliage pushes up from the mulch, and daylily leaves can be as tall as crows. Buds on the daffodils foretell the next season of flowering bulbs and the deepening of Early Spring. Bobwhites call. Great flocks of starlings and grackles move across the nation as February comes to an end. And from now on, average temperatures rise at their spring and early summer rate, one degree every three days.

Daybook

1981: First red knuckles of peonies pushing up from the ground.

1983: Star of Holland foliage is up two inches at the corner of Dayton and High. Daffodils six inches there.

1984: Crocus blooming at Jane Morgan's in the Vale.

1985: Cardinal sings at 6:54 a.m., four minutes earlier than on the 18th. This afternoon at South Glen: The river is high with snowmelt, and everything is growing back: Jacob's ladder, spring beauties, wood mint, henbit, catchweed, violet cress, moneywort, waterleaf, sweet rockets, leafcup, hemlock, parsnip, garlic mustard. Some multiflora roses have leaves. Skunk cabbage is red, fat, and blooming in the swamp flats.

1987: Two daffodils with buds in front of the bookstore downtown.

1989: Robins, cardinals, doves, blue jays loud at eight o'clock. Flock of starlings and some crows come to the back at 9:30.

1993: More deep freeze, almost a foot of snow on the ground.

1995: Walk in the yard this Sunday morning. The sky hazy, air mild in the low 50s, cardinals singing all around. In the south garden, the first tulips are up, yarrow and mallow just starting to come back, sweet rockets strong, daffodils four or five inches tall, yellow, gold and violet snow crocus and snowdrops in bloom. Under the cherry tree, new tulip bulbs planted last fall are just emerging. Along the north side of the yard, new Dutch leaves are more than half a foot high, and the first dandelion is open among the sweet Williams. In the east garden, snow crocus, snowdrops in bloom, stonecrop has started to come back, iris pushing out a little.

1996: First snow crocus buds appear in the mild afternoon. Snowdrops are ready.

1998: Out pruning in the south garden and south hedge: I saw Resurrection lilies up an inch, and the first of the early purple iris had bloomed yesterday in the cherry tree garden circle. Crows and cardinals and flickers loud while I worked in the mild morning, sun through the filter of cirrus clouds overhead, south wind. Pond water is at 53 degrees; the fish still huddle at the bottom. In a pale violet crocus in the east garden, the first honey bee of the year, its legs full of pollen. First dandelion open in the back yard.

1999: Crocus season continues through the long cold spell.

2000: At 5:00 this mild morning, I stood and listened to the whinny of the screech owl that lives near Limestone Street. The interval was regular for the first few minutes I listened, about every 20 seconds. Then the whinnies came farther apart, and I could barely make out a return call off to the north, jumbled in the sound of the cars on the freeway five miles away. At 6:52 a.m., as I walked out to the truck, a cardinal sang, and then a dove. On the way back from work in the afternoon, I saw maples flowering. When I got home from the hospital, the first spring iris had blossomed, dark purple, all the snow crocus were in full bloom, daffodils were budding, hyacinths coming up, some tulip foliage three inches tall. No crows seen on my commute. They seem to have left their winter congregation, split up into smaller groups for mating and summer.

2003: Driving to Washington Court House today in the cold and snow, I started encountering small flocks robins about six miles south of town. I kept seeing them as I passed through Cedarville and Jamestown and then on to the freeway. I felt as though I were in the middle of a great spring flock that stretched at least twenty miles across the white, hostile landscape.

2005: More snow crocus, maybe a dozen plants, have emerged in the east and south gardens. Even with the temperature near 35 this afternoon, some of the purples were open. Snowdrops continue full bloom. A few more red peony stalks have pushed up through the mulch, are about a half an inch tall now. When I stopped at the drug store, I saw Mike Tripplett; he said he had seen red-winged blackbirds in Kentucky yesterday and that they must have followed him home – they were singing in his yard this morning.

2007: A screech owl was calling this morning at 6:00. At 6:45, cardinals were singing. A little later, I heard mourning doves for the first time before dawn. Tonight, I went out to get firewood, and I heard the screech owl again.

2009: Driving across eastern Texas: deep drought throughout the area. Some greening of a few short, thin shrubs, but the maple seeds have disappeared, and the land is dominated by scrub evergreens. Even the cacti have turned brown from lack of water. By the motel, one small white cress plant with palmate basal leaves and shepherd's purse-type seeds in bloom. In Kerrville for repairs. From Yellow Springs, Mike reports red-winged blackbirds.

2010: Snow cover remains, but a faint odor of skunk tonight.

2011: A little snow cover here, but half a foot not far to the north. Crows at 6:50, cardinals, house sparrows, a field sparrow, and grackles singing throughout my walk with Bella at 9:00.

2012: Bright sun and chilly, cardinal called at 6:48 this morning.

2017: Reckless Early Spring: Until the arrival of Snowdrop Winter on February 25, Early Spring had come head-over-heels into the Glen and Yellow Springs. After a January six degrees above average and a remarkable February (at this writing) over eleven degrees above average, the land responded with change most likely not seen since the warmest January-February on record in 1890.

The thaw began with a record high temperature of 66 degrees on February 18. Many daffodils were budded that morning, and snowdrops, aconites and snow crocuses were in full bloom, pussy willows about half emerged; tulips and hyacinths and even a couple of peony shoots were up three inches. After the sun burned away the fog on the 20th, the first mosquito of South High Street came in my open porch door and attacked.

One of the most remarkable events occurred on the 21st. The morning was mild, 52 degrees before sunup. I went out about 6:30 listening for cardinals. A small tan moth flew away into the dooryard garden as I went down the steps. There were no birds until 6:47, and then I heard a robin whinny. Two minutes later, a robin singsong call, the first of the robin-mating chorus for the year. Ordinarily, robins do not sing before the first or second week of March, and the earliest I had recorded it before was March 2 of 2011.

Throughout the day, a flock of grackles (that often arrive back in Yellow Springs with the robins) appeared at my feeder. Violet crocus were opening all over town – a whole yard of them on Walnut Street. In the afternoon, I found the very first blue squill of the year, outrider of daffodils.

February 22: A fifth mild day: The robin chorus was underway once again when I went outside a little after 7:00. Leaves were emerging on the lower honeysuckle branches in the Glen. A precocious white hepatica was in flower along the river. In the alley at home, I found the first henbit and bittercress blooming, and forsythia buds were ready to open along the street..

The 23rd brought a record high of 69 degrees. Robins were in their mating chorus when I went outside at 6:38. Ed showed me a deep-purple iris reticulata on his property. In front of the post office, stonecrop foliage was about three inches high. At home, many forsythia flowers came fully open, one daffodil tried to unravel, some standard crocuses bloomed, white and purple. Peony, daffodil and hyacinth stalks were surging, a few more squills showing. Boxwood, red quince, multiflora rose bushes and Japanese honeysuckle were leafing

The 24th was the last and the warmest day of this February heat wave (with a record high of 76 degrees). Three daffodils opened all the way overnight; two more came in throughout the day, and this was ten days earlier than I had recorded the first daffodil since I started keeping records.

More mosquitoes were flying in the afternoon, small moths and ichneumons in the woods. I found maples in bloom, some already shedding their flowers. Pussy willows were all white against the blue sky. The first cabbage butterfly flew across my dooryard garden; the earliest I had seen one before was March 8 of 1983.

And Chris even told me he heard peeping spring peepers, maybe the earliest they had peeped around here (according to my weather history) since the hot winter of 1890.

2018: Sun and crisp, frost on the car, snow crocus blooming all around the yard, daffodils surging, ramps three inches, cardinals singing, honeysuckle buds greening, the circle garden full of green hyacinth and daffodil and allium spears. Small "sweat bees" (genus: *Agpostemon)* seen working the dry flower stalks in the sun. Casey called in the afternoon to report that a murder of crows was attacking a black buzzard in a tree on Whiteman Street.

2019: Clear and 20s at dawn: doves at 6:40, crows at 6:44, cardinals at 6:45, and when I got home from my walk with Ranger, I was greeted by a loud robin in the dooryard (but no robin chorus so far). From Indianapolis, Emily reports hundreds of sandhill cranes flying northwest around noon, showing, once again, the synchronicity of February grackles, red-winged blackbirds, robins and sandhills. And in Yellow Springs, Leslie and Bruce heard a killdeer today. (The average arrival date in Dayton is the 22nd.)

2020: Overcast and 33 degrees, snow expected. The first cardinal sang at 6:52 this morning, and then the whole neighborhood of cardinals came into song. Later in the day, I noticed that stonecrop/sedum foliage had begun to emerge from the mulch by the back porch.

2021: High 20s, mostly clear skies: Cardinals, doves, song sparrows, Carolina chickadees and a robin in song when I went outside to walk Ranger at 6:50 this morning. Almond trees in Italy are in full bloom, Neysa reports.

2022: A dusting of snow in the night, doves calling in the cold. Ice on the maple and honeysuckle branches shines like brilliant planets and stars against the blue sky.

2023: Pussy willow catkins bright and crisp against clear blue sky. Daffodil count well underway: One dozen blooms today. At last light, I heard a soft dialogue between to screech owls.

Before a tip of green showed in any brushy place you could feel spring growing through the sky. The robins came early, cocking heads in the cold. The gray bodies of the goldfinches yellowed, for all the world like pussy buds blooming. And where no other sign held on wood or field, finger twigs of elder and willow and service swelled beneath their hull of bark.

James Still

February 27th
The 58th Day of the Year

See the Spring brings back its pleasures,
all the passions of its treasures,
and the sun calls out the flowers,
soothes the meadow with its colors,
plucks the sadness from the gray,
and from the wildness of the Winter day.

From the Carmina Burana
(bf)

Sunrise/set: 7:12/6:24
Day's Length: 11 hours 12 minutes
Average High/Low: 42/24
Average Temperature: 33
Record High: 70 – 1996
Record Low: - 2 – 1963

Weather
The weather often begins to moderate again, with a ten percent chance of highs in the 50s, and a 35 percent chance of 40s. Cooler temperatures are also common, however: a 35 percent chance of 30s and a 20 percent chance of a high in the 20s. Rain or snow falls three days out of a decade on this date. If there is to be a seventh cold wave this month, it strikes today or tomorrow. Four years in ten, however, it doesn't come to Ohio at all.

Natural Calendar
Maple Syrup Season, Snowdrop and Aconite Season, and Pussy Willow Season continue (or begin) in cooler years, have ended in the mildest years. Daffodil Budding Season and Crocus Blooming Season commence. Migration Season peaks for Canadian geese. Walleye, Sauger, Saugeye, Muskie, Bass and Crappie Feeding Seasons gets underway. Earthworm Mating Season has begun in warming rains. Foliage Growing Season accelerates, with leaves of wild violets and honeysuckles appearing as March approaches.

1987: Snowdrops are budding by the peach tree. Aconite opens two petals. Hemlock to six inches by the Covered Bridge. After a dry January and February, the river is low. Do migrations of suckers and carp wait until the rush of warming waters from the spring rains, the breakup of ice, spring flooding, ancient cues to movement and courtship?

1992: Silver maples flower in the triangle park on Dayton Street.

1993: Two more inches of snow yesterday. South Glen is white, the river frozen along the banks, all the way across in some places. The progress of the first two weeks of the month has been covered by the cold of last two, even the cardinals singing less, the sparrows less boisterous. Looking back: The years 1980, 1984, and 1986 were like this at the end of February. The last six years, though, the final weeks of the month have been mild.

1994: Walking Buttercup up to the park at about 8:30 this morning, I counted 35 robins sitting under the crabapple trees eating fruit, their feathers fluffed. In the south garden, celandine and poppies are showing some signs of life, despite the frozen ground. Some daffodils are up two inches.

1996: Today is the first dramatic day of Early Spring, a record high of 70 degrees, several clumps of gold and violet snow crocus and one snowdrop opened. Since the cold ended on the 19th, daffodils and tulips have come up two inches in most places, new lily foliage beside them, and the garlic planted in November is growing. On the way home from school, I almost hit a woolly bear caterpillar crossing the road, and Jeanie said one of the kindergartners brought in a woolly bear, too. Taking the garbage cans out to the street this afternoon, I pushed the leaves away from the ground, discovered a night crawler lying in the dirt.

1998: When I walked out the door today, a mourning cloak butterfly flew down High Street in front of our forsythia. Along Wilberforce-Clifton Road: flocks of red-winged blackbirds and robins in the fields, and a maple flowering. Waterleaf is up in the garden and at South Glen, clovers and grasses growing, more garlic mustard sprouting, flickers calling.

1999: Thunderstorm this morning, I found a fat worm lying near the back porch, forced out of his lair by the water.

2000: The fish in our pond are sluggish but continue to move around. Swamp iris foliage has come out of the water two to three inches.

2004: Cardinals and doves were singing when I let the dog out the back door at 6:43 this morning. Casey phoned at a little after 10:00 last Saturday morning: "I'm sitting here with John Bush by the old lumber yard," he said, "and we're watching five buzzards just circling up there catching the first thermal of the day." Casey and I talked for a few more minutes, then he added, "Now there are some more coming in – two more up there now!"

Other birds are affirming the buzzards' optimism. Along the Little Miami River, geese are looking for nesting sites. A pair of pileated woodpeckers has been visiting the wooded lots along Dayton Street, according to Greg. More signs of spring accumulate. Most snowdrops, yellow aconites, and many purple and gold snow crocus bloomed during the last few days. Greg stopped by, holding his hands about six inches apart. "The daffodils at my house are this tall," he said with a big smile.

2005: The temperature was in the teens this morning, only reached into the 30s this afternoon. The sap was slow at Antioch School, but the bright yellow crocus in the south garden opened for a little while when the sun came out this afternoon.

2006: Inventory in the yard: Daffodils four to six inches – some budded, hyacinths two inches, peonies an inch and a half, full snow crocus, aconites and snowdrops, daylilies three inches, tulips three inches, most pussy willows cracked, mats of purple deadnettle growing.

2007: Cardinal heard at 6:44 a.m. Snow still covers all the gardens, even though the highs have been in the 30s for several days.

2009: Kerrville, Texas: Walking along the Guadeloupe River in downtown Kerrville, temperature in the high 80s: the ground so dry it crinkled under foot. We saw a full-blooming redbud tree, and all the tall trees that lined the water (I believe cottonwoods) were budded.

2011: Crows and cardinals before 7:00 this morning, most all the last snow having melted overnight, a deep thaw moving up from the south, rain and rain and flooding predicted for this afternoon and tonight. In the sun around noon: the very first snow crocus are opening, hellebore buds are opening, a few daffodils are budded, the first sedum foliage has emerged. At Clifton Gorge, foliage of the wild sedum, hepatica, violet cress, zigzag goldenrod, and leafcup showing. Winged, termite-like insects were crawling around on a fallen tree.

Casey reports hearing red-winged blackbirds, and Liz saw sandhill cranes: "I saw a flock of eight flying from the South East to the North West this morning about 10:20 a.m. I first heard geese, and very high up was a skein of them, which I was watching (from the corner of Philips and Davis, walking with Mattie), and then I heard the cranes. At first I couldn't see them, because they were in my line of vision with the sun, but eventually they flew right overhead, also fairly high up. Awesome!"

2012: To Knoxville, Tennessee: The landscape unchanged throughout most of the trip. We had left Yellow Springs at the height of the first blooming of Early Spring, full aconites, snow crocus, snowdrops, pussy willows and budding daffodils. We saw the first daffodils open near Berea, Kentucky and then another few patches before we stopped for the night north of Knoxville. No flowering trees noticed along the way.

2016: It is getting to be March, and the sun comes more and more directly into my office window and into the window to the green bedroom where Jeanie and I slept for thirty-eight years. And now the worst of the winter seems over, the first thaw of Early Spring moving in (which will not be shattered so completely with cold like the winter thaws), bright sun, a forecast for highs in the upper 40s, and the snowdrops will open again, and the snow crocus, and more crocus will emerge and bud and bloom. Tonight, a mosquito, the first I've seen so far this year, bothered me as I made my list for tomorrow.

2017: Even as the weather becomes chillier, the daffodil buds grow larger. I found ramps foliage up four inches by the mock orange bush.

2018: The first squill opening by the southwest garden, the first of my aconites in the circle garden, the first leaves out on the lower branches of one honeysuckle bush, flowers on silver maples, all the aconites in full bloom in front of the house on South Stafford Street, the sky so clear blue all day, Monk the cat basking in the old grass. From Goshen, Indiana, this morning, Judy reports that the red-winged blackbirds are back at her pond, a few days earlier than in previous years. At 3:05 this afternoon, Aida called: "Bluebirds, bluebirds, bluebirds," she said, "all over Allen Street by the Antioch forest and our property on the Allen Street side."

2019: A small flock of robins conversing along my block of High Street about 7:00 this morning, but no chorus. In the back yard before noon, four grackles feeding, the first to come to the yard this winter. In the west porch garden, autumn sedum is about an inch high. Along Dayton Street, two of Don's daffodils have tight buds close to the ground. Leslie and Bruce saw a slight gilding on the a male goldfinch. Tat reports sandhill cranes passing through Madison, Wisconsin. Judy in Goshen, Indiana, has geese on her pond for the first time this year; the pairing has begun.

2021: Rain and mild this morning, cardinals, doves and chickadees at 6:48, a few robins in the streets around the neighborhood, some robin whinnies after 7:00.

From Spoleto, Italy, Neysa sent photos of *Cornus mas* in full bloom by her house and of what appears to be a kind of *Pyrola grandiflora* or *Foglia rotunda* with fat, fleshy basal leaves and spikes of purple-pink flowers. Neysa wrote a little later to say Ivano identified it as a *Bergenia crassifolia.*

Emily sends an update: "With this 50° day there is the arrival of Redwing blackbirds in the fields, joining the flocks of grackles and starlings. And little snow drops are popping out of the ground at my sit spot on S. College St.! My friend in the Vale also reports having snow drops and aconites, but in full bloom."

And Michele writes from the Flying Mouse Farm: "Here's a twist this year. Every year that we have made syrup the Grade A Golden is always the first syrup we get no matter when the sap flows. This year the first sap that we got is definitely Grade A Amber. No way we can say its Golden. Weird! I just thought you might be interested. I hope it's a fluke and not a trend. Actually the Golden is probably the least favored in our area, and the amber is what most people like. However, I'm just afraid if it's a trend, it might be yet another sign of climate change. Recent research has suggested we probably only have about 30 more years of syrup making in this part of Ohio."

2022: Snowdrop Winter melts in the sun, cloudless skies, and yesterday's high ice, still shining, drops and clashes with the ice below, tiny shooting stars. Jack Blakelock sends two haikus from Walnut Street:

Uppermost branches
etched in silver (rising sun)
ice-storm's memory.

A breeze and sunlight,
trees' frozen armors relax
come clattering down.

Can you ever be sure that you have heard the very first wood frog in the township croak?

Henry David Thoreau

Sunrise/set: 7:10/6:26
Day's Length: 11 hours 16 minutes
Average High/Low: 42/25
Average Temperature: 33
Record High: 64 – 1972
Record Low: - 3 – 1934

Weather

The sun shines more often on February 28th than on any other February day in my record: 80 percent of the years are partly or mostly clear. Rain comes just 20 percent of the days, snow only five to ten percent. Although there is a 20 percent chance of a high only in the 20s or teens, that is balanced by a 25 percent chance of a high in the 50s. The remaining highs are evenly divided between 30s and 40s. It is unlikely that morning lows will fall below zero.

Natural Calendar

In February, if the days be clear,
The waking bee, still drowsy on the wing,
Will guess the opening of another year
And blunder out to seek another spring.

Vita Sackville-West

An inventory in the first weeks of Early Spring offers a measure for the year and a record against which to compare the Late Winter of other years. Measure the height of hyacinths, daffodils and tulips. Note the color and size of lilac and other buds. Count the number of pussy willows emerged. Look for new leaves on garlic mustard and poppies. Check for chickweed greening in the bushes. The longer the list of plants observed in February inventory, the greater the context for observing the subtle alterations in each day to come, the more exciting each addition.

Daybook

1983: First moth seen at the front window.

1985: Geese fly over the house. Fern Albertson reports that the first crocus opened in her yard.

1986: Cardinal sings at 6:50 a.m., 20 minutes before sunrise, three degrees above zero and clear. In the greenhouse, mother-of-millions continues to bloom.

1988: Robin killed flying into a window at Wilberforce.

1990: First fly in the office.

1991: First red-winged blackbird seen along Wilberforce-Clifton Road, the earliest I've ever sighted one there. First aconite blooms in the yard.

1992: The warmest winter in local history: December 1991 through February 1992.

1993: Sun, high pressure system peaking, the last of the high winter tides. Cardinals, crows, starlings, sparrows, doves strong this morning. From Jacksonville, Jeni says some of the trees in her protected courtyard are leafing out; the canopy through the city, though, hasn't started to fill in. Outside here in the snow, a couple of rabbits have left tracks across the yard, and a mouse, burrowing out from under a drift by the stone rose fence, has explored all the way to the house and back. At Jacoby, I was able to walk through the cattail swamp for first time across the ice. The woods was quiet except for a kingfisher west toward the river, an occasional crow, the tapping of a woodpecker. A half-dozen sparrows were hopping in and around the shallow water of the swamp, finding seeds or insects among the cress plants. Despite the whiteness and the snow, there was no sense of winter; the air was mild and the sun almost hot.

1998: More spring: Chives and blue flags are up two inches or so, pacing each other; thousands of new craneflies spin by the garden wall; cardinals and doves are singing by 6:35 in the morning; the full chorus including geese and the rattles of woodpeckers is underway by 7:15. And the first mosquito came to the back screen this afternoon.

1999: Crows and cardinals by 6:45 a.m. Warm, cloudy. At 7:30, there is really a chorus of cardinals and crows and titmice filling the morning space with sound.

2000: A lot of daffodils budding along the front sidewalk; one of them might still bloom in February.

2004: Daffodils in the yard are only up about three inches. One clump of purple crocus has been blooming in the south garden since maybe the 26th.

2008: Jacoby: Snow still was several inches thick on most of the hillsides, but the streams, as always, remained open. Deer tracks were prominent, their paths leading to the watercress – areas of which showed signs of having been pulled up and eaten. Skunk cabbage was open in many places throughout the swamp; in snowy areas, the cabbage has opened a passage for itself, emerging thanks to its own heat. Up the talus slope, blue jays were calling. Crows cawed overhead. Today in the yard, the finches continued to feed, their bodies brightening slowly. Titmice and cardinals sang throughout the morning and afternoon. Grackles and starlings worked the suet and remaining seed. This evening, Al and Donna Denman wrote to say they had seen their first mallard pair in Birch Creek today.

2009: Kerrville, Texas to Big Bend National Park along the Rio Grande: Another redbud seen in bloom, this one along I-10. From the Hill Country, we entered the bare approach down from the freeway, and then the mountains of the park appeared in the south. Along the road, several large yuccas in bloom, Joshua trees or *Yucca brevifolia.* Yellow fruit noticed on segmented cactus, probably *Tasajillo* cactus. Texas bluebonnets prominent along the roadside inside the park. At the campground, acacias are in full bloom, their orange puffball flowers dominating the area.

2010: Cardinal sang at 6:45 this morning. Three juncos seen near the pond at noon.

2011: The first thunderstorm of the year came through last night. Casey saw the first male red-winged blackbird at his pond this morning, and he said that yesterday the honeybees were all over his aconite, "I mean a lot of bees!" Walking Bella in the alley this morning, I found Katie's aconites in full early bloom.

2012: Knoxville, Tennessee to Jekyll Island, Georgia: Sun and warm throughout the drive, the first maples flowering halfway to Asheville, all the daffodil beds in full early bloom through the mountains. First flowering cherry or plum trees - a large planting of them near Spartanburg, occasional white flowering shrubs down through the foothills, bright yellow jessamine about an hour northwest of Columbia and many more white-flowering shrubs, and more and more red maple flowers. A black swallowtail at the Georgia line and another a little later. Along the road to Jekyll, white clover, ragwort-type plants and even a redbud in bloom.

On the island: Warm in the 70s. Numerous butterflies seen: two sulphurs, a buckeye, a yellow tiger swallowtail, a cabbage white and even a monarch. Many azaleas had started, and the gardenia-like shrub at the bookstore here was in full bloom. Along the dunes, creeping blackberries, dandelion, lavender-like plants, great white thistles, black medic, sow thistle and several other *compositae* noticed.

When we reached our motel, I checked my messages: Casey had called at 10:30 that morning: "Red-winged blackbirds at the pond," he said.

2015: Walking Bella this morning at 9:00, I heard blue jays and doves for the first time this year.

2016: In town, many golden crocuses (first day at Jill's) opening now, and mid-season purples. In the north garden, Tulips planted last year send up their swarthy spikes, older tulips leafing. Spiderwort, Shasta daisy and day lilies have one to two inch leaves. Clusters of stonecrop foliage. A fly has joined the many Asian lady beetles in Jill's house, and we saw a pair of honking geese flying over East Enon Road.

Yesterday, Jill and I interrupted a pair of geese that were nestled in a fold of Clifton Gorge. They had been in raucous conversation, became quiet as we approached, had settled down with their beaks under their wings. Throughout the late afternoon and evening, I was overcome with a spring garden nostalgia, all the new growth making me feel lonely without Jeanie.

On the 29th, cloudy, light wind, 39 degrees: A full range of birdsong, prelude to the Great Chorus: A cardinal sang as I came out the door this morning at 6:43. Doves joined in along High Street at 6:53, occasional "pee wee" calls, robin whinnies and peeps from then on, song sparrows at 6:58, then crows at 7:00. Before 7:15: house sparrows, a blue jay, a pair of geese flying over. In the afternoon, in the low 50s, Ed Oxley called: At his property, he had dozens of honeybees, a lot of newborn flies, blooming scilla, buds on a few daffodils and grape hyacinths getting tall. His dog even found a garter snake in the sun!

2017: A strong thunderstorm in the late afternoon.

2018: Rain approaching. Peter Hayes says he has moles digging through his lawn. Midseason crocuses are now full at Liz's house and here.

2019: A strong high-pressure system is approaching, and new moon in a few days will keep spring back a week or two. But Judy reports hearing red-winged blackbirds at her place in Goshen, Indiana, and Tat and Maggie saw a flock of sandhills flying over in Madison, Wisconsin. At Ellis Pond, the number of geese is down to maybe a third of what it was a month ago, about 150 total now in three separate flocks. Still no robin chorus here, and no crocuses yet, either. The month's average was 34.8 degrees, 3.8 above normal. And the rainfall was 6.15 inches, 3.91 inches above normal.

2020: Clear and cold in the teens. Cardinals and doves strong throughout the neighborhood at 6:40 this morning. Once again as I walked the alley between High and Stafford Streets, the chickadee gave its "Hey, Sweetie" mating call, a clear two/three-note song, the first note higher than the second. The call is so clear that it seems to be that of a black-capped chickadee, but it's more likely that of a Carolina chickadee, a species more common here. On the 29th, Mary Sue reports her first red-winged blackbirds of the year.

The average temperature this month was 33.6 degrees, 2.6 degrees above normal; precipitation was 2.71 inches, just a little above average.

2021: A warm rain throughout the night, all but a few mounds of snow gone. Walking at 7:20, I watched a pair of geese fly over, the first pair I've seen this year. Yesterday, there were still hundreds of geese gathered at the pond, but it seems the pairing off has begun. I noticed that one Lenten rose blossom had opened as the snow melted. And tonight, walking Ranger, I smelled my first skunk of the year in the soft wind.

The average temperature this month was 25.9 degrees, a little more than five degrees below normal. Total precipitation was below two inches, but snowfall was 16 inches, well above average.

2022: Sun and frost. Red-shouldered hawk flies over this morning as I stack wood. Casey left a message this afternoon: red-winged blackbirds "picking at the peanuts" in his feeders. At Clifton Gorge, Jill and I heard geese honking down in the gorge near the river (like in 2016). In the lawn near the feeders this evening, three robins. This month's average temperature was 32.8, about a degree above average. Precipitation was 2.35 inches, snowfall 6.6 inches.

2023: After yesterday's storm, red maples buds on Stafford Street, marking the GDD of about 40 for the end of the month this year. In 2017, with a February slightly warmer than this year's, the red maples fell on Stafford Street on the 25th. All of about a fourth of the aconites in the alley behind the old Danielsons' house have faded. The robin chorus still going at about 8:30 this morning. The monthly temperature average: 40.7 as of today, eight degrees above normal, according to the NOAA record. The Ohio State phenology report says that the whole month of February produced 68 GDD in Springfield; the heuristic system of GDD produces only background or parallel information to the daybook, a lot of calculation for a relatively cloudy outcome not much more useful than backyard records.

At the end of the first month of spring, the yang ethers of heaven are said to waft down while the yin ethers of earth arise. They commingle harmoniously, and as a result grasses and trees begin to sprout.... In spring, nature reconnects the two existential essences and everything surges back to life.

Liza Dalby

Journal

And so we see in Plants and all of Nature the Word of God. Like any Scripture, Earth's Matter is subject to our Doubt. But to the one who listens closely to its Cadence, it reveals the sweet hidden Truth.

Reginald Johnson, *On the Shapes of Leaves*, 1697

For many years, I have kept track of the waves of barometric pressure that pass over my Ohio home. I have compared their configurations on my graphs and have found similarities in the rises and the falls of the pressure from year to year. These resemblances are consistent enough to produce reliable weather history forecasts, which can predict likely conditions on any day of the year.

While I have done little with my graphs but reinvent the wheel first discovered by 16th century almanackers, I have been surprised that modern meteorology has been so reluctant to embrace barometric regularity as a means of long-range forecasting. Recent research on the *El Nino* phenomena is the first sign that academic meteorologists are beginning to take atmospheric rhythms seriously.

Post-chaos theory physicists (who belong to what has been called the "Universal" school) are also looking at patterns in nature and have come up with notions that support the ancient use of barometric patterning in tracking and predicting likely weather scenarios. In the late 1970s, an IBM research scientist named Benoit Mandelbrot looked at fluctuations in all kinds of phenomena, from the stock market to cloud formations. He came to the conclusion that these very different occurrences were related to one another, and that they revealed an underlying force that pervaded every aspect of life on earth.

In each of the events he studied, Mandelbrot found "self-similar" systems, which he called fractals. It is probably easier to picture a fractal than to define it. Imagine an electrocardiograph analysis of your heartbeat. The ups and downs are arranged on the paper in an orderly fashion, but never at exactly the same intervals. Or picture a month or two of a graph of the Down Jones averages. That's a fractal pattern. Although a weather graph of temperature or barometric pressure may chart very different activities and show much greater variability than the electrocardiograph record (and is much less depressing than a stock market graph), Mandelbrot would posit that all of the records are showing us a life principle, not unlike a yin-yang law, that underlies not only weather, stocks, and heartbeats but almost everything from the shape of ferns and fiords to the filigree in lungs and leaves.

That there is a relationship between heart rhythms, barometric rhythms, temperature rhythms, and the patterns of clouds, the stock market, and even shape of frost on the windshield of my truck in winter is apparently not a matter of too much debate, at least among post-chaos theory physicists who belong to this "universal" school. All of the systems mentioned can be charted as fractals, and a visual analysis of their designs reveals their broad similarity.

The real issue, however, is whether the designs have meaning. If fractals reflect some universal designing set in nature, and if they are, in fact, the signatures of nature, then what are we to make of them?

During the Middle Ages, the Doctrine of Signatures held that the shape of any natural object, such as a leaf or root, held the key to its medicinal use. Thus, the hepatica leaf, reminiscent of the shape of a human liver, indicated its application in the treatment of liver ailments. Modern fractal theory posits a not so dissimilar view – that patterns observed in such diverse phenomena as the stock market and barometric pressure might not only hold the key to understanding the rhythm but also the ultimate meaning of those phenomena. Some analysts believe that fractals could hold the secret key to the universe, explain the causes not only of our personal decisions but of the outside forces that influence them. Science writer Mark Ward even conjectures that fate itself might be fractal.

In organizing barometric patterns from the past quarter century, I have found that my charts allow for weather predictions which are unavailable from any other source. This practical aspect of fractal records is intriguing to me less for its meteorological implications, however, than for its psychological implications. Always eager to jump to conclusions, I wonder what new fractal highs and lows remain to be discovered, and I wonder if they will really tell us the "sweet hidden Truth" promised by Reginald Johnson in 1697.

Bill Felker has been writing *Poor Will's Almanack* for newspapers and magazines since 1984, and he has published annual almanacs since 2003. His radio version of *Poor Will* is broadcast weekly on WYSO, a National Public Radio station, and it is available on podcast at www.wyso.org. He has published three collections of his columns, *Home is the Prime Meridian: Essays in Search of Time and Place, Deep Time Is in the Garden: New Essays in Search of Time and Place and Spirit,* and *The Virgin Point: Meditations in Nature.* Those books and the entire twelve volumes of *A Daybook for the Year in Yellow Springs* are available on Amazon.

For   more   information,   visit   Bill   Felker's   website   at **www.poorwillsalmanack.com**